Praise for *Marketing Insights from A to Z*

"The bagwan of Marketing strikes again. Leave it to Phil Kotler to revisit all of our blocking and tackling at just the right time . . . and as all great marketers know: 'timing is everything.'"

> —Watts Wacker
> Founder and CEO, FirstMatter
> Author, *The Deviant Advantage: How Fringe Ideas Create Mass Markets*

"Wide-ranging, readable, pithy, and right on target, these insights not only are a great refresher for marketing managers but should be required reading for all nonmarketing executives."

> —Christopher Lovelock
> Adjunct Professor, Yale School of Management
> Author, *Services Marketing*

"Kotler tackles the formidable challenge of explaining the entire world of marketing in a single book, and, remarkably, pulls it off. This book is a chance for you to rummage through the marketing toolbox, with Kotler looking over your shoulder telling you how to use each tool. Useful for both pros and those just starting out."

> —Sam Hill
> Author, *Sixty Trends in Sixty Minutes*

"This storehouse of marketing wisdom is an effective antidote for those who have lost sight of the basics, and a valuable road map for those seeking a marketing mind-set."

> —George Day
> Geoffrey T. Boisi Professor of Marketing,
> Wharton School of Business

"Here is anything and everything you need to know about where marketing stands today and where it's going tomorrow. You can plunge into this tour de force at any point from A to Z and always come up with remarkable insights and guidance. Whatever your position in the business world, there is invaluable wisdom on every page."

> —Stan Rapp
> Coauthor, *MaxiMarketing and Max-e-Marketing in the Net Future*

"A nourishing buffet of marketing wisdom. This is a book to which you will return many times after the initial reading."

> —Leonard Berry
> Distinguished Professor of Marketing,
> Texas A&M University
> Author, *Discovering the Soul of Service*

Marketing Insights
from A to Z

Marketing Insights
from A to Z

80 Concepts Every Manager Needs To Know

Philip Kotler

John Wiley & Sons, Inc.

Library of Congress Cataloging-in-Publication Data:
Kotler, Philip.
   Marketing insights from A to Z : 80 concepts every manager needs
   to know / Philip Kotler.
     p. cm.
  ISBN 0-471-26867-4
  1. Marketing. I. Title.
  HF5415 .K63127 2003
  658.8—dc21   2002014903

Printed in the United States of America.

10 9 8 7 6 5 4 3 2

To all those who have worked in
business and marketing
with a passion to satisfy customer needs
and enhance customer and societal well-being.

Preface

My 40-year career in marketing has produced some knowledge and even a little wisdom. Reflecting on the state of the discipline, it occurred to me that it is time to revisit the basic concepts of marketing.

First, I listed the 80 concepts in marketing critical today and spent time mulling over their meanings and implications for sound business practice. My primary aim was to ascertain the best principles and practices for effective and innovative marketing. I found this journey to be filled with many surprises, yielding new insights and perspectives.

I didn't want to write another 800-page textbook on marketing. And I didn't want to repeat thoughts and passages that I have written in previous books. I wanted to present fresh and stimulating ideas and perspectives in a format that could be picked up, sampled, digested, and put down anytime. This short book is the result, and it was written with the following audiences in mind:

- Managers who have just learned that they need to know something about marketing; you could be a financial vice president, an executive director of a not-for-profit organization, or an entrepreneur about to launch a new product. You may not even have time to read *Marketing for Dummies* with its 300 pages. Instead you want to understand some key concepts and marketing principles presented by an authoritative voice, in a convenient way.

- Managers who may have taken a course on marketing some years ago and have realized things have changed. You may want to refresh your understanding of marketing's essential concepts and need to know the latest thinking about high-performance marketing.
- Professional marketers who might feel unanchored in the daily chaos of marketing events and want to regain some clarity and recharge their understanding by reading this book.

My approach is influenced by Zen. Zen emphasizes learning by means of meditation and direct, intuitive insights. The thoughts in this book are a result of my meditations on these fundamental marketing concepts and principles.

Whether I call these meditations, ruminations, or cogitations, I make no claim that all the thoughts in this book are my own. Some great thinkers in business and marketing are directly quoted, or they directly influenced the thoughts here. I have absorbed their ideas through reading, conversations, teaching, and consulting.

Introduction

Today's central problem facing business is not a shortage of goods but a shortage of customers. Most of the world's industries can produce far more goods than the world's consumers can buy. Overcapacity results from individual competitors projecting a greater market share growth than is possible. If each company projects a 10 percent growth in its sales and the total market is growing by only 3 percent, the result is excess capacity.

This in turn leads to hypercompetition. Competitors, desperate to attract customers, lower their prices and add giveaways. These strategies ultimately mean lower margins, lower profits, some failing companies, and more mergers and acquisitions.

Marketing is the answer to how to compete on bases other than price. Because of overcapacity, marketing has become more important than ever. Marketing is the company's *customer manufacturing department*.

But marketing is still a terribly misunderstood subject in business circles and in the public's mind. Companies think that marketing exists to help manufacturing get rid of the company's products. The truth is the reverse, that manufacturing exists to support marketing. A company can always outsource its manufacturing. What makes a company prosper is its marketing ideas and offerings. Manufacturing, purchasing, research and development (R&D), finance, and other company functions exist to support the company's work in the customer marketplace.

Marketing is too often confused with selling. Marketing and selling are almost opposites. "Hard-sell marketing" is a contradiction. Long ago I said: **"Marketing is not the art of finding clever ways to dispose of what you make. Marketing is the art of creating genuine customer value. It is the art of helping your customers become better off. The marketer's watchwords are quality, service, and value."**

Selling starts only when you have a product. Marketing starts before a product exists. Marketing is the homework your company does to figure out what people need and what your company should offer. Marketing determines how to launch, price, distribute, and promote your product/service offerings to the marketplace. Marketing then monitors the results and improves the offering over time. Marketing also decides if and when to end an offering.

All said, marketing is not a short-term selling effort but a long-term investment effort. When marketing is done well, it occurs before the company makes any product or enters any market; and it continues long after the sale.

Lester Wunderman, of direct marketing fame, contrasted selling to marketing in the following way: **"The chant of the Industrial Revolution was that of the manufacturer who said, 'This is what I make, won't you please buy it?' The call of the Information Age is the consumer asking, 'This is what I want, won't you please make it?' "**[1]

Marketing hopes to understand the target customer so well that selling isn't necessary. Peter Drucker held that **"the aim of marketing is to make selling superfluous."**[2] **Mark**-eting is the ability to hit the **mark.**

Yet there are business leaders who say, "We can't waste time on marketing. We haven't designed the product yet." Or "We are too successful to need marketing, and if we were unsuccessful, we couldn't afford it." I remember being phoned by a CEO: "Come and teach us some of your marketing stuff—my sales just dropped by 30 percent."

Here is my definition of marketing: **Marketing management is the art and science of choosing target markets and getting, keeping, and growing customers through creating, communicating, and delivering superior customer value.**

Or if you like a more detailed definition: **"Marketing is the business function that identifies unfulfilled needs and wants, defines and measures their magnitude and potential profitability, determines which target markets the organization can best serve, decides on appropriate products, services, and programs to serve these chosen markets, and calls upon everyone in the organization to think and serve the customer."**

In short, marketing's job is to convert people's changing needs into profitable opportunities. Marketing's aim is to create value by offering superior solutions, saving buyer search and transaction time and effort, and delivering to the whole society a higher standard of living.

Marketing practice today must go beyond a fixation on transactions that often leads to a sale today and a lost customer tomorrow. The marketer's goal is to build a mutually profitable long-term relationship with its customers, not just sell a product. A business is worth no more than the lifetime value of its customers. This calls for knowing your customers well enough to deliver relevant and timely offers, services, and messages that meet their individual needs.

The function of marketing is typically organized as a department within a business. This is good and bad. It's good because it brings together a number of skilled people with specific abilities for understanding, serving, and satisfying customers. It's bad because other departments believe that all marketing is done in one department. As the late David Packard of Hewlett-Packard observed, **"Marketing is much too important to leave to the marketing department. . . . In a truly great marketing organization, you can't** tell who's in the marketing department. Everyone in the organization has to make decisions based on the impact on the customer."

The same thought was well-stated by Professor Philippe Naert: **"You will not obtain the real marketing culture by hastily creating a marketing department or team, even if you appoint extremely capable people to the job. Marketing begins with top management. If top management is not convinced of the need to be customer minded, how can the marketing idea be accepted and implemented by the rest of the company?"**

Marketing is not restricted to a department that creates ads, selects media, sends out direct mail, and answers customer questions. Marketing is a larger process of systematically figuring out what to make, how to bring it to the customer's attention and easy access, and how to keep the customer wanting to buy more from you.

Furthermore, marketing strategy and actions are not only played out in customer markets. For example, your company also has to raise money from investors. As a result you need to know how to market to investors. You also want to attract talent to your company. So you need to develop a value proposition that will attract the most able people to join your company. Whether marketing to customers, investors, or talent, you need to understand their needs and wants and present a competitively superior value proposition to win their favor.

Is marketing hard to learn? The good news is that marketing takes a day to learn. The bad news is that it takes a lifetime to master! But even the bad news can be looked at in a positive way. I take inspiration from Warren Bennis' remark: "Nothing gives me a greater joy than learning something new." (Mr. Bennis is Distinguished Professor at the University of California and prominent writer on leadership.)

The good news is that marketing will be around forever. The bad news: It won't be the way you learned it. In the coming decade, marketing will be reengineered from A to Z. I have chosen to highlight 80 of the most critical concepts and ideas that businesspeople need in waging their battles in this hypercompetitive and rapidly changing marketplace.

Contents

Advertising   1

Brands   8

Business-to-Business Marketing   15

Change   16

Communication and Promotion   18

Companies   20

Competitive Advantage   22

Competitors   23

Consultants   25

Corporate Branding   26

Creativity   27

Customer Needs   30

Customer Orientation   32

Customer Relationship Management (CRM)   34

Customers   36

Customer Satisfaction   41

Database Marketing   43

Design   46

Differentiation 49

Direct Mail 52

Distribution and Channels 53

Employees 57

Entrepreneurship 60

Experiential Marketing 61

Financial Marketing 62

Focusing and Niching 64

Forecasting and the Future 66

Goals and Objectives 68

Growth Strategies 70

Guarantees 74

Image and Emotional Marketing 76

Implementation and Control 77

Information and Analytics 80

Innovation 83

Intangible Assets 86

International Marketing 87

Internet and E-Business 91

Leadership 94

Loyalty 97

Management 99

Marketing Assets and Resources 101

Marketing Department Interfaces 102

Marketing Ethics 106

Marketing Mix 108

Marketing Plans 112

Marketing Research 115

Marketing Roles and Skills 119

Markets	**121**
Media	**123**
Mission	**124**
New Product Development	**126**
Opportunity	**128**
Organization	**130**
Outsourcing	**131**
Performance Measurement	**133**
Positioning	**135**
Price	**138**
Products	**140**
Profits	**142**
Public Relations	**145**
Quality	**147**
Recession Marketing	**149**
Relationship Marketing	**151**
Retailers and Vendors	**154**
Sales Force	**157**
Sales Promotion	**160**
Segmentation	**162**
Selling	**164**
Service	**167**
Sponsorship	**169**
Strategy	**171**
Success and Failure	**175**
Suppliers	**176**
Target Markets	**177**
Technology	**178**
Telemarketing and Call Centers	**179**

xviii Contents

Trends in Marketing Thinking and Practice **181**

Value **183**

Word of Mouth **185**

Zest **187**

Notes **189**

Index **195**

Advertising

I (and most people) have a love/hate relationship with advertising. Yes, I enjoy each new Absolut vodka print ad: Where will they hide the famous bottle? And I enjoy the humor in British ads, and the risqué quality of French ads. Even some advertising jingles and melodies stick in my mind. But I don't enjoy most ads. In fact, I actively ignore them. They interrupt my thought processes. Some do worse: They irritate me.

The best ads not only are creative, they sell. Creativity alone is not enough. Advertising must be more than an art form. But the art helps. William Bernbach, former head of Doyle, Dane & Bernbach, observed: **"The facts are not enough. . . . Don't forget that Shakespeare used some pretty hackneyed plots, yet his message came through with great execution."**

Even a great ad execution must be renewed or it will become outdated. Coca-Cola cannot continue forever with a catchphrase like "The Real Thing," "Coke Is It," or "I'd Like to Teach the World to Sing." Advertising wear-out is a reality.

Advertising leaders differ on how to create an effective ad campaign. Rosser Reeves of the Ted Bates & Company advertising agency favored linking the brand directly to a single benefit, as in

"R-O-L-A-I-D-S spells RELIEF." Leo Burnett preferred to create a character that expressed the product's benefits or personality: the Green Giant, the Pillsbury Doughboy, the Marlboro cowboy, and several other mythical personalities. The Doyle, Dane & Bernbach agency favored developing a narrative story with episodes centered on a problem and its outcome: thus a Federal Express ad shows a person worried about receiving something at the promised time who is then reassured by using FedEx's tracking system.

The aim of advertising is not to state the facts about a product but to sell a solution or a dream. Address your advertising to the customers' aspirations. This is what Ferrari, Tiffany, Gucci, and Ferragamo do. A Ferrari automobile delivers on three dreams: social recognition, freedom, and heroism. Remember Revlon founder Charles Revson's remark: "In our factory, we make lipstick. In our advertising, we sell hope."[3]

But the promise of dreams only makes people suspicious of advertising. They don't believe that their selection of a particular car or perfume will make them any more attractive or interesting. Stephen Leacock, humorist and educator, took a cynical view of advertising: **"Advertising may be described as the science of arresting the human intelligence long enough to get money from it."**

Ads primarily create product awareness, sometimes product knowledge, less often product preference, and more rarely, product purchase. That's why advertising cannot do the job alone. Sales promotion may be needed to trigger purchase. A salesperson might be needed to elaborate on the benefits and close the sale.

What's worse, many ads are not particularly creative. Most are not memorable. Take auto ads. The typical one shows a new car racing 100 miles an hour around mountain bends. But we don't have mountains in Chicago. And 60 miles an hour is the speed limit. And furthermore I can't remember which car the ad featured. Conclusion: Most ads are a waste of the companies' money and my time.

Most ad agencies blame the lack of creativity on the client.

Clients wisely ask their agencies to come up with three ads, from mild to wild. But then the client typically settles for the mild and safe one. Thus the client plays a role in killing good advertising.

Companies should ask this question before using advertising: **Would advertising create more satisfied clients than if our company spent the same money on making a better product, improving company service, or creating stronger brand experiences?** I wish that companies would spend more money and time on designing an exceptional product, and less on trying to psychologically manipulate perceptions through expensive advertising campaigns. **The better the product, the less that has to be spent advertising it.** The best advertising is done by your satisfied customers.

The stronger your customer loyalty, the less you have to spend on advertising. First, most of your customers will come back without you doing any advertising. Second, most customers, because of their high satisfaction, are doing the advertising for you. In addition, advertising often attracts deal-prone customers who will flit in and out in search of a bargain.

There are legions of people who love advertising whether or not it works. And I don't mean those who need a commercial to provide a bathroom break from the soap opera. My late friend and mentor, Dr. Steuart Henderson Britt, passionately believed in advertising. **"Doing business without advertising is like winking at a girl in the dark. You know what you are doing, but nobody else does."**

The advertising agency's mantra is: "Early to bed, early to rise, work like hell, advertise."

But I still advise: Make good advertising, not bad advertising. David Ogilvy cautioned: **"Never write an advertisement which you wouldn't want your own family to read. You wouldn't tell lies to your own wife. Don't tell them to mine."**[4]

Ogilvy chided ad makers who seek awards, not sales: **"The advertising business . . . is being pulled down by the people who** create it, who don't know how to sell anything, who have never sold anything in their lives . . . who despise selling, whose mission in life is to be clever show-offs, and con clients into giving them money to display their originality and genius."[5]

Those who love advertising can point to many cases where it worked brilliantly: Marlboro cigarettes, Absolut vodka, Volvo automobiles. It also worked in the following cases:

- A company advertised for a security guard. The next day it was robbed.
- If you think advertising doesn't pay—we understand there are 25 mountains in Colorado higher than Pikes Peak. Can you name one?

Those against too much reliance on advertising are fond of quoting John Wanamaker of department store fame: **"I know that half the money I spend on advertising is wasted; but I can never find out which half."**

How should you develop your advertising? You have to make decisions on the five Ms of advertising: *mission, message, media, money,* and *measurement.*

The ad's *mission* can be one of four: to **inform, persuade, remind,** or **reinforce** a purchase decision. With a new product, you want to inform and/or persuade. With an old product, like Coca-Cola, you want to remind. With some products just bought, you want to reassure the purchaser and reinforce the decision.

The *message* must communicate the brand's distinctive value in words and pictures. Any message should be tested with the target audience using a set of six questions (see box).

The *media* must be chosen for their ability to reach the target market cost-effectively. Besides the classic media of newspapers, magazines, radio, television, and billboards, there is a flurry of new media, including e-mail, faxes, telemarketers, digital magazines, in-store ad-

---

Advertisement Message Test

1. What is the main message you get from this ad?
2. What do you think the advertiser wants you to know, believe, or do?
3. How likely is it that this ad will influence you to undertake the implied action?
4. What works well in the ad and what works poorly?
5. How does the ad make you feel?
6. Where is the best place to reach you with this message—where would you be most likely to notice it and pay attention to it?

---

vertising, and advertising now popping up in skyscraper elevators and bathrooms. Media selection is becoming a major challenge.

A company works with the media department of the ad agency to define how much *reach*, *frequency*, and *impact* the ad campaign should achieve. Suppose you want your advertising campaign to deliver at least one exposure to 60 percent of the target market consisting of 1,000,000 people. This is 600,000 exposures. But you want the average person to see your ad three times during the campaign. That is 1,800,000 exposures. But it might take six exposures for the average person to notice your ad three times. Thus you need 3,600,000 exposures. And suppose you want to use a high-impact media vehicle costing $20 per 1,000 exposures. Then the campaign should cost $72,000 ($20 × 3,600,000/1,000). Notice that your company could use the same budget to reach more people with less frequency or to reach more people with lower-impact media vehicles. There are trade-offs among reach, frequency, and impact.

Next is *money*. The *ad budget* is arrived at by pricing the reach, frequency, and impact decisions. This budget must take into account that the company has to pay for ad production and other costs.

A welcome trend would be that advertisers pay advertising agencies on a pay-for-performance basis. This would be reasonable because the agencies claim that their creative ad campaigns will increase the companies' sales. So pay the agency an 18 percent commission if sales increase, a normal 15 percent commission if sales remain the same, and a 13 percent commission with a warning if sales have fallen. Of course, the agency will say that other forces caused the drop in sales and even that the drop would have been deeper had it not been for the ad campaign.

Now for *measurement*. Ad campaigns require premeasurement and postmeasurement. Ad mock-ups can be tested for communication effectiveness using recall, recognition, or persuasion measures. Postmeasurements strive to calculate the communication or sales impact of the ad campaign. This is difficult to do, though, particularly with image ads.

For example, how can Coca-Cola measure the impact of a picture of a Coke bottle on the back page of a magazine on which the company spent $70,000 to influence purchases? At 70 cents a bottle and 10 cents of profit per bottle, Coke would have to sell 700,000 additional bottles to cover the $70,000 cost of the ad. I just don't believe that ad will sell 700,000 extra bottles of Coke.

Companies must try, of course, to measure results of each ad medium and vehicle. If online promotions are drawing in more prospects than TV ads, adapt your budget in favor of the former. Don't maintain a fixed allocation of your advertising budget. Move ad money into the media that are producing the best response.

One thing is certain: Advertising dollars are wasted when spent to advertise inferior or indistinct products. Pepsi-Cola spent $100 million to launch Pepsi One, and it failed. In fact, the quickest way to kill a poor product is to advertise it. More people will try the product sooner and tell others faster how bad or irrelevant it is.

How much should you spend on advertising? If you spend too little, you are spending too much because no one notices it. A million dollars of TV advertising will hardly be noticed. And if you spend too many millions, your profits will suffer. Most ad agencies push for a "big bang" budget and while this may be noticed, it hardly moves sales.

It is hard to measure something that can't be measured. Stan Rapp and Thomas Collins put their finger on the problem in the book *Beyond MaxiMarketing*. **"We are simply emphasizing that research often goes to great lengths to measure irrelevant things, including people's *opinions* about advertising or their *memories* of it rather than their *actions* as a result of it."**[6]

Will mass advertising diminish in its influence and use? I think so. People are increasingly cynical about and increasingly inattentive to advertising. One of its former major spenders, Sergio Zyman, ex-vice president of Coca-Cola, said recently, **"Advertising, as you know it, is dead."** He then redefined advertising: **"Advertising is a lot more than just television commercials—it includes branding, packaging, celebrity spokespeople, sponsorships, publicity, customer service, the way you treat your employees, and even the way your secretary answers the phone."**[7] What he is really doing is defining marketing.

A major limitation of advertising is that it constitutes a monologue. As evidence, most ads do not contain a telephone number or e-mail address to enable the customer to respond. What a lost opportunity for the company to learn something from a customer! Marketing consultant Regis McKenna observed: **"We are witnessing the obsolescence of advertising. The new marketing requires a feedback loop; it is this element that is missing from the monologue of advertising."**[8]

rands

Everything is a brand: Coca-Cola, FedEx, Porsche, New York City, the United States, Madonna, and you—yes, you! A brand is any label that carries meaning and associations. **A great brand does more: It lends coloration and resonance to a product or service.**

Russell Hanlin, the CEO of Sunkist Growers, observed: **"An orange is an orange . . . is an orange. Unless . . . that orange happens to be Sunkist, a name 80 percent of consumers know and trust."** We can say the same about Starbucks: "There is coffee and there is Starbucks coffee."

Are brands important? Roberto Goizueta, the late CEO of Coca-Cola, commented: **"All our factories and facilities could burn down tomorrow but you'd hardly touch the value of the company; all that actually lies in the goodwill of our brand franchise and the collective knowledge in the company."** And a booklet by Johnson & Johnson reaffirms this: **"Our company's name and trademark are by far our most valuable assets."**

Companies must work hard to build brands. David Ogilvy insisted: **"Any damn fool can put on a deal, but it takes genius, faith and perseverance to create a brand."**

The sign of a great brand is how much loyalty or preference it commands. Harley Davidson is a great brand because Harley Davidson motorcycle owners rarely switch to another brand. Nor do Apple Macintosh users want to switch to Microsoft.

A well-known brand fetches extra pennies. The aim of branding, according to one cynic, "is to get more money for a product than it is worth." But this is a narrow view of the benefits that a trusted brand confers on users. The user knows by the brand name the product quality and features to expect and the services that will be rendered, and this is worth extra pennies.

A brand saves people time, and this is worth money. Niall Fitzgerald, chairman of Unilever, observed: **"A brand is a storehouse of trust that matters more and more as choices multiply. People want to simplify their lives."**

The brand amounts to a contract with the customer regarding how the brand will perform. The brand contract must be honest. Motel 6, for example, offers clean rooms, low prices, and good service but does not imply that the furnishings are luxurious or the bathroom is large.

How are brands built? It's a mistake to think that advertising builds the brand. Advertising only calls attention to the brand; it might even create brand interest and brand talk. Brands are built *holistically*, through the orchestration of a variety of tools, including *advertising*, *public relations (PR)*, *sponsorships*, *events*, *social causes*, *clubs*, *spokespersons*, and so on.

The real challenge is not in placing an ad but to get the media talking about the brand. Media journalists are on the lookout for interesting products or services, such as Palm, Viagra, Starbucks, eBay. A new brand should strive to establish a new category, have an interesting name, and tell a fascinating story. If print and TV will pick up the story, people will hear about it and tell their friends. Learning about a brand from others creates credibility. Learning about it only through paid advertising is easy to dismiss because of the biased nature of advertising.

Don't advertise the brand, live it. Ultimately the brand is built by your employees who deliver a positive experience to the customers. Did the *brand experience* live up to the *brand promise*? This is why companies must orchestrate the brand experience with the brand promise.

Choosing a good brand name helps. A consumer panel was shown the pictures of two beautiful women and asked who was more beautiful. The vote split 50–50. Then the experimenter named one woman Jennifer and the other Gertrude. The woman named Jennifer subsequently received 80 percent of the votes.

Great brands are the only route to sustained, above-average profitability. And great brands present emotional benefits, not just rational benefits. Too many brand managers focus on rational incentives such as the brand's features, price, and sales promotion, which contribute little to growing the brand-customer relationship. Great brands work more on emotions. And in the future, great brands will show social responsibility—a caring concern for people and the state of the world.

A company needs to think through what its brand is supposed to mean. What should Sony mean, Burger King mean, Cadillac

Richard Branson's Virgin brand is about fun and creativity. These attributes are projected in all of Virgin's marketing activities. Some of Virgin Atlantic's Airways' flights include massages, live rock bands, and casinos. Flight attendants are fun-loving and enjoy joking with the passengers. Branson uses public relations to project his daring, such as attempting to fly around the world in a hot-air balloon. To launch Virgin Bride (bridal wear), Branson dressed up in drag as a bride.

mean? A brand must be given a personality. It must thrive on some trait(s). And the traits must percolate through all of the company's marketing activities.

Once you define the attribute(s) of your brand, you need to express them in every marketing activity. Your people must live out the brand spirit at the corporate level and at the job-specific level. Thus if your company brands itself as innovative, then you must hire, train, and reward people for being innovative. And being innovative must be defined for every job position, including the production supervisor, the van driver, the accountant, and the salesperson.

The brand personality must be carried out by the company's partners as well. The company cannot allow its dealers to compromise the brand by engaging in price-cutting against other dealers. They must represent the brand properly and deliver the expected brand experience.

When a brand is successful, the company will want to put the brand name on additional products. The brand name may be put on products launched in the same category (*line extension*), in a new category (*brand extension*), or even in a new industry (*brand stretch*).

Line extension makes sense in that the company can coast on the goodwill that it has built up in the category and save the money that it would otherwise have to spend to create brand awareness of a new name and offering. Thus we see Campbell Soup introducing new soups under its widely recognized red label. But this requires the discipline of adding new soups while subtracting unprofitable soups from the line. The new soups can cannibalize the sales of the core soups without bringing in much additional revenue to cover the additional costs. They can reduce operational efficiency, increase distribution costs, confuse consumers, and reduce overall profitability. Some line extensions are clearly worth adding, but overuse of line extensions must be avoided.

Brand extension is riskier: I buy Campbell's soup but I might be less interested in Campbell's popcorn. *Brand stretch* is even more risky: Would you buy a Coca-Cola car?

Well-known companies tend to assume that their great name

can carry them successfully into another category. Yet whatever happened to Xerox computers or Heinz salsa? Did the Hewlett-Packard/Compaq iPAQ Pocket PC overtake the Palm handheld or did Bayer acetaminophen overtake Tylenol? Is Amazon electronics as successful as Amazon books? Too often the company is introducing a me-too version of the product that ultimately loses to the existing category leaders.

The better choice would be to establish a new name for a new product rather than carry the company's name and all of its baggage. The company name creates a feeling of more of the same, rather than something new. Some companies know this. Toyota chose not to call its upscale car Toyota Upscale but rather Lexus; Apple Computer didn't call its new computer Apple IV but Macintosh; Levi's didn't call its new pants Levi's Cottons but Dockers; Sony didn't call its new videogame Sony Videogame but PlayStation; and Black & Decker didn't call its upgraded tools Black & Decker Plus but De-Walt. Creating a new brand name gives more opportunity to establish and circulate a fresh public relations story to gain valuable media attention and talk. A new brand needs credibility, and PR is much better than advertising in establishing credibility.

Yet every rule has its exceptions. Richard Branson has put the name Virgin on several dozen businesses, including Virgin Atlantic Airways, Virgin Holidays, Virgin Hotels, Virgin Trains, Virgin Limousines, Virgin Radio, Virgin Publishing, and Virgin Cola. Ralph Lauren's name is found on numerous clothing products and home furnishings. Still a company has to ask: How far can the brand name be stretched before it loses its meaning?

Al Ries and Jack Trout, two keen marketing thinkers, are against most line and brand extensions; they see it as diluting the brand. To them, a Coke should mean an eight-ounce soft drink in the famous Coke bottle. But ask today for a Coke and you will have to answer whether you want Coca-Cola Classic, Caffeine Free Coca-Cola Classic, Diet Coke, Diet Coke with Lemon, Vanilla Coke, or

Cherry Coke—and do you want it in a can or a bottle? Vendors used to know what you wanted when you asked for a Coke.

Brand pricing is a challenge. When Lexus started to make inroads against Mercedes in the United States, Mercedes wasn't going to lower its price to match Lexus' lower price. No, some Mercedes managers even proposed raising Mercedes' price to establish that Mercedes is selling prestige that the buyer can't get from a Lexus.

But brand price premiums today are shrinking. A leading brand in the past could safely charge 15 to 40 percent more than the average brand; today it would be lucky to get 5 to 15 percent more. When product quality was uneven, we would pay more for the better brand. Now all brands are pretty good. Even the store's brand is good. In fact, it probably is made by the national brand to the same standards. So why pay more (except for show-off brands like Mercedes) to impress others?

In recessionary times, price loyalty is greater than brand loyalty. Customer loyalty may reflect nothing more than inertia or the absence of something better. As someone observed, "There is nothing that a 20 percent discount won't cure."

A company handles its brands through brand managers. But Larry Light, a brand expert, doesn't think that brands are well managed. Here is his plaint: **"Brands do not have to die. They can be murdered. And the marketing Draculas are draining the very lifeblood away from brands. Brands are being bargained, belittled, bartered and battered. Instead of being brand-asset managers, we are committing brand suicide through self-inflicted wounds of excessive emphasis on prices and deals."**

Another concern is that brand management structures may militate against carrying out effective customer relationship management (CRM) practices. Companies tend to overfocus and overorganize on the basis of their products and brands, and underfocus on managing their customers well. Call it *brand management myopia.*

Heidi and Don Schultz, marketing authors, believe that the consumer packaged goods (CPG) model for brand building is increasingly inappropriate, especially for service firms, technology firms, financial organizations, business-to-business brands, and even smaller CPG companies.[9] They charge that the proliferation of media and message delivery systems has eroded mass advertising's power. They urge companies to use a different paradigm to build their brands in the New Economy.

- Companies should clarify the corporation's basic values and build the corporate brand. Companies such as Starbucks, Sony, Cisco Systems, Marriott, Hewlett-Packard, General Electric, and American Express have built strong corporate brands; their name on a product or service creates an image of quality and value.
- Companies should use brand managers to carry out the tactical work. But the brand's ultimate success will depend on everyone in the company accepting and living the brand's value proposition. Prominent CEOs—such as Charles Schwab or Jeff Bezos—are playing a growing role in shaping brand strategies.
- Companies need to develop a more comprehensive brand-building plan to create positive customer experiences at every touch point—events, seminars, news, telephone, e-mail, person-to-person contact.
- Companies need to define the brand's basic essence to be delivered wherever it is sold. Local executions can be varied as long as they deliver the feel of the brand.
- Companies must use the brand value proposition as the key driver of the company's strategy, operations, services, and product development.
- Companies must measure their brand-building effectiveness not by the old measures of awareness, recognition, and recall, but by a more comprehensive set of measures including customer perceived value, customer satisfaction, customer share of wallet, customer retention, and customer advocacy.

Business-to-Business Marketing

Most marketing is business-to-business (B2B) marketing even though textbooks and business magazines devote most of their attention to business-to-consumer (B2C) marketing. The disproportionate attention to B2C has been justified by saying that (1) B2C is where most of modern marketing concepts first arose, and (2) B2B marketers can learn a lot by adopting B2C thinking. While these two statements are true, B2B is having its own renaissance, and maybe B2C marketers have a lot to learn from B2B practices. B2B, in particular, has focused more on individual customers, and B2C is increasingly moving into one-to-one customer thinking.

The sales force is the main driver in B2B marketing. Its importance cannot be overestimated, especially when selling complex customized equipment such as B-47s or power plants or selling to large national and global accounts. Today's companies increasingly assign national and global *account managers* to manage their largest customers. Account management systems will grow in the future as more of the world's business becomes concentrated in fewer but larger companies.

But today B2B companies also are driven to replace high-cost sales calls with less expensive contact channels such as tele- and videoconferencing and Web-based communications, where possible.

As videoconferencing improves and costs come down, companies will reduce the number of field visits to customers and save on the high costs of transportation, hotels, dining out, and entertaining.

Another force that might reduce the role of the sales force is the growth of Web-based market exchanges. Price differences—especially for commodity materials and components—will become more visible, thus making it harder for salespeople to influence buyers to pay more than the market price. (See Sales Force and Selling.)

hange

Change, not stability, is the only constant. Companies today have to run faster to stay in the same place. Some say that if you remain in the same business, you will be out of business. Note that companies such as Nokia and Hewlett-Packard gave up their original businesses. Survival calls for self-cannibalization.

Your company has to be able to recognize Strategic Inflection Points, defined by Andy Grove of Intel as **"a time in the life of a business when its fundamentals are about to change."** Banks had to make changes with the advent of automated teller machines (ATMs), and major airlines have to make changes with the new competition coming from low-fare airlines.

Jack Welch at GE admonished his people: **"DYB: Destroy your** business. . . . **Change or die. When the rate of change inside the company is exceeded by the rate of change outside the company, the end is near."**

Tom Peters' advice: **"To meet the demands of the fast-changing competitive scene, we must simply learn to love change as much as we hated it in the past."**

I have noticed that American and European businesspeople respond differently to change. Europeans see it as posing a threat. Many Americans see it as presenting opportunities.

The companies that fear change most are many of today's leading companies. As incumbents, they have invested so much in their present tangible assets that they tend to either ignore or fight the insurgents. Because they are big, they think they are built to last. But being big is no guarantee against becoming irrelevant, as Kmart, A&P, and Western Union discovered. If companies don't want to be left behind, they must anticipate change and lead change. The ability to change faster than your competitors amounts to a competitive advantage.

Richard D'Aveni, the author of *Hypercompetitive Rivalries*,[10] observed: **"In the end, there will be just two kinds of firms: those who disrupt their markets and those who don't survive the assault."**

But how do you change a company? How do you get your employees to adopt a new mind-set and give up their comfortable activities and learn new ones? Clearly top management must develop a new compelling vision and mission whose benefits for the various stakeholders appear far greater than the risk and cost of change. Top management must gather support and apply *internal marketing* to produce change in the organization.

The best defense in the face of change is to create a company that thrives on change. The company would see change as normal rather than as an interruption of the normal. And it would attract people who have positive attitudes toward change. It would institute open discussions of policy, strategy, tactics, and organization. The worst thing is to be a company that dislikes change. Such a company will attract people who dislike change, and the end is inevitable.

As Reinhold Niebuhr stated: "God, give us grace to accept with serenity the things that cannot be changed, courage to change the things that should be changed, and the wisdom to distinguish the one from the other."

Communication and Promotion

Among the most important skills in marketing are communication and promotion. *Communication* is the broader term, and it happens whether planned or not. A salesperson's attire communicates, the catalog price communicates, and the company's offices communicate; all create impressions on the receiving party. This explains the growing interest in *integrated marketing communications (IMC)*. Companies need to orchestrate a consistent set of impressions from its personnel, facilities, and actions that deliver the company's brand meaning and promise to its various audiences.

Promotion is that part of communication that consists of company messages designed to stimulate awareness of, interest in, and purchase of its various products and services. Companies use advertising, sales promotion, salespeople, and public relations to disseminate messages designed to attract attention and interest.

Promotion cannot be effective unless it catches people's attention. But today we are deluged with print, broadcast, and electronic information. We confront 2 billion Web pages, 18,000 magazines, and 60,000 new books each year. In response, we have developed routines to protect ourselves from information overload. We toss most catalogs and direct mail unopened into the wastebasket; delete unwanted and unread e-mail messages; and refuse to listen to telephone solicitations.

Thomas Davenport and John Beck point out in *The Attention Economy* that the glut of information is leading to attention deficit disorder (ADD), the difficulty of getting anyone's attention.[11] The attention deficit is so pronounced that companies have to spend more money marketing than making the product. This is certainly the case with new perfume brands and many new films. Consider that the makers of *The Blair Witch Project* spent $350,000 making the film and $11 million to market it.

As a result, marketers need to study how people in their target market allocate their attention time. Marketers want to know the best way to get a larger share of consumers' attention. Marketers apply attention-getting approaches such as high-profile movie stars and athletes; respected intermediaries close to the target audience; shocking stories, statements, or questions; free offers; and countless others.

Even then, there is a question of effectiveness. It is one thing to create awareness, another to draw sustained attention, and still another to trigger action. Attention is to get someone to spend time focusing on something. But whether this leads to buying action is another question.

Companies

It has been observed that there are four types of companies:

1. Those that make things happen.
2. Those that watch things happen and respond.
3. Those that watch things happen and don't respond.
4. Those that didn't notice that anything had happened.

No wonder the average company disappears within 20 years. Of the companies listed as best in the Forbes 100 of 1917, only 18 survived to 1987. And only two of them, General Electric and Eastman Kodak, were making good money.

And not all existing companies are truly alive. Companies fool us by merely breathing day to day. General Motors and Sears have been losing shares for years even though their hearts are still ticking. You can enter some companies and tell within 15 minutes whether they are alive or dead, just by looking at the employees' faces.

I no longer know what a large company is. Company size is relative. Boeing, Caterpillar, Ford, General Motors, Kellogg, Eastman Kodak, J. P. Morgan, and Sears are giant companies. But in early

2000 Microsoft Corporation achieved a market value that exceeded that of all eight companies combined.

What makes some companies great? There's a whole string of books ready to tell us the answer. Tom Peters and Bob Waterman started the guessing game with *In Search of Excellence* in 1982.[12] Of the 70 companies they nominated, many are moribund today. Then we heard from Jim Collins and Jerry Porras in *Built to Last* (1994),[13] Michael Treacy and Fred Wiersema in *The Discipline of Market Leaders* (1995),[14] Arie De Geus in *The Living Company* (1997),[15] and most recently from Jim Collins again in *Good to Great: Why Some Companies Make the Leap . . . and Others Don't* (2001).[16]

These books point out the many correlations of successful companies. But I have a simple thesis: Companies last as long as they continue to provide superior customer value. They must be market-driven and customer-driven. In the best cases, they are market-driving. They create new products that people may not have asked for but afterwards thank them for. Thanks to Sony for your Walkman, your smaller storage disks, your incredible camcorders, and your innovative computers.

Customer-oriented companies make steady gains in mind share and heart share, leading to higher market shares and in turn to higher profit shares.

Tom Siebel, CEO of Siebel Systems, has a simple but comprehensive view of what creates great companies. **"Focus on satisfying your customers, becoming a market leader, and being known as a good corporate citizen and a good place to work. Everything else follows."** (See Customer Orientation.)

Competitive Advantage

Michael Porter popularized the notion that a company wins by building a relevant and sustainable competitive advantage.[17] Having a competitive advantage is like having a gun in a knife fight.

This is true, but today most advantages don't stay relevant and few are sustainable. Advantages are temporary. Increasingly, a company wins not with a single advantage but by layering one advantage on top of another over time. The Japanese have been masters at this, first coming in with low prices, then with better features, then with better quality, and then with faster performance. The Japanese have recognized that marketing is a race without a finishing line.

Companies can build a competitive advantage from many sources, such as superiority in quality, speed, safety, service, design, and reliability, together with lower cost, lower price, and so on. It is more often some unique combination of these, rather than a single silver bullet, that delivers the advantage.

A great company will have incorporated a set of advantages that all reinforce each other around a basic idea. Wal-Mart, IKEA, and Southwest Airlines have unique sets of practices that enable them to charge the lowest prices in their respective industries. A competitor that copies only a few of these practices will not succeed in gaining an advantage.

Recognize that competitive advantages are relative, not absolute.

If the competition is improving by 30 percent and you by 20 percent, you are losing competitive advantage. Singapore Airlines kept improving its quality, but Cathay Pacific was improving its quality faster, thereby gradually closing the gap with Singapore Airlines.

Competitors

All firms have competitors. Even if there were only one airline, the airline would have to worry about trains, buses, cars, bicycles, and even people who might prefer to walk to their destinations.

The late Roberto Goizueta, CEO of Coca-Cola, recognized Coke's competitors. When his people said that Coke's market share was at a maximum, he countered that Coca-Cola accounted for less than 2 ounces of the 64 ounces of fluid that each of the world's 4.4 billion people drank every day. **"The enemy is coffee, milk, tea, water,"** he told his people. Coca-Cola is now a major seller of bottled water.

The more success a company has, the more competition it will attract. Most markets are brimming with whales, barracudas, sharks, and minnows. In these waters, the choice is to eat lunch or be lunch. Or, using computer scientist Gregory Rawlins' metaphor: **"If you're not part of the steamroller, you're a part of the road."**

Hopefully your company will attract only good competitors. Good competitors are a blessing. They are like good teachers who raise our sights and sharpen our skills. Average competitors are a nuisance. Bad competitors are a pain to every decent competitor.

A company should never ignore its competitors. Stay alert. "Time spent in reconnaissance is seldom wasted," noted Sun Tzu in the fourth century B.C. And your *allies* should stay alert. If you are going to be an effective competitor, you must also be an effective *co-operator*. You are not a solo business but a partnership, a network, an extended enterprise. Competition today is increasingly between networks, not companies. And your ability to spot faster, learn faster, and work faster as a network is a key competitive advantage.

In the short run, the most dangerous competitors are those that resemble your company the most. The customers can't see the difference. Your company is a toss-up in their mind. So differentiate, differentiate, differentiate.

According to marketing guru Theodore Levitt: "The new competition is not between what companies produce in their factories, but between what they add to their factory output in the form of packaging, services, advertising, customer advice, financing, delivery arrangements, warehousing, and other things that people value."[18]

The way to beat your competitors is to attack yourself first. Work hard to make your product line obsolete before your competitors do.

Watch your distant competitors as well as your close ones. My guess is that your company is more likely to be buried by a new disruptive technology than by nasty look-alike competitors. Most fatal competition will come from a small competitor who burns with a passion to change the rules of the game. IBM made the mistake of worrying more about Fujitsu than a nobody named Bill Gates who was working on software in his garage.

As important as it is to watch your competitors, it is more important to obsess on your customers. Customers, not competitors, determine who wins the war. Most markets are plagued by too many fishermen going after too few fish. The best fishermen understand the fish better than their competitors do.

Consultants

Consultants can play a positive role in helping companies reappraise their market opportunities, strategies, and tactics. Consultants provide a client company with an outside-in view to correct the company's tendency to take an inside-out view.

Yet some managers say: "If we are successful, we don't need consultants. If we are unsuccessful, we can't afford them."

We need fewer *consultants* and more *resultants*. Too many consultants give you advice and fail to grapple with the difficult problem of implementing the recommendations. Keep the consultant and pay him or her according to results.

Here is a test for finding a good consultant. Ask each consultant, "What time is it?"

- The first consultant says: "It is exactly 9:32 A.M. and 10 seconds." Hire him if you want an accurate, fact-filled study.
- The second consultant answers: "What time do you want it to be?" Hire him if you don't want advice so much as corroboration.
- The third consultant answers: "Why do you want to know?" Hire him if you want some original thinking, such as defin-

ing the problem more carefully. Peter Drucker says that his greatest strength as a consultant is to be ignorant and ask a few basic questions.

There is a lot of cynicism about consultants. As early as the first century B.C., Publilius Syrus, a Latin writer, noted: **"Many receive advice, few profit by it."** Robert Townsend, former CEO of Avis Rent-A-Car, described consultants as **"people who borrow your watch and tell you what time it is and then walk off with the watch."** William Marsteller, of Burson-Marsteller public relations, added: **"A consultant is a person who knows nothing about your business to whom you pay more to tell you how to run it than you could earn if you ran it right instead of the way he tells you."**

The cynicism simply means that there are good and bad consultants and your task is to be able to tell the difference.

Corporate Branding

There is great payoff in building a strong corporate brand. Sony can put its name on any electronic device and customers will prefer it to the competition. Virgin can enter almost any business and be successful because its name means brings a fresh approach to that business.

The major requirement for corporate branding is for the company to stand for something, whether it is quality, innovation, friendliness, or something else. Take Caterpillar, the heavy construction equipment manufacturer. Caterpillar's brand personality triggers such associations as hardworking, resilient, tough, bold, and determined. So Caterpillar has been able to launch Cat jeans, sandals, sunglasses, watches, and toys, all designed with the same traits in mind.

A strong corporate brand needs good image work in terms of a theme, tag line, graphics, logo, identifying colors, and advertising dollars. But the company shouldn't overrely on an advertising approach. Corporate image is more effectively built by company performance than by anything else. Good company performance plus good PR will buy a lot more than corporate advertising.

Creativity

Companies formerly won their marketing battles through superior efficiency or quality. Today they must win through superior creativity. One does not win through *better sameness*; one wins through *uniqueness*. Winning companies such as IKEA, Harley Davidson, and Southwest Airlines are unique.

Uniqueness requires developing a culture that honors creativity. There are three ways to increase your company's creativity:

1. Hire more naturally creative people and give them free rein.
2. Stimulate creativity in your organization through a myriad of well-tested techniques.

3. Contract for creativity help. Go to Brighthouse in Atlanta, Faith Popcorn in New York, or Leo Burnett in Chicago, for example, and get help in finding a breakthrough idea.

See the box for descriptions of some of the leading creativity techniques that can be used in-house.

Creativity Techniques

- *Modification analysis.* With respect to some product or service, consider ways to adapt, modify, magnify, minify, substitute, rearrange, reverse, or combine.
- *Attribute listing.* Define and modify the attributes of the product. For example, in seeking to build a better mousetrap, consider ways to improve bait, method of execution, method of hearing execution, method of removal, shape, material, price.
- *Forced relationships.* Try out new combinations. For example, in trying to build a new type of office furniture, consider combining a desk and a bookcase, or a bookcase and a filing system.
- *Morphological analysis.* Play with the basic dimensions of the problem. For example, in trying to move something from one point to another, consider the type of vehicle (cart, chair, sling, bed), the medium in which/by which the vehicle operates (air, water, oil, rollers, rails), and the power source (compressed air, engine, steam, magnetic field, cable).
- *Product problem analysis.* Think of all the problems that a specific product has. For example, chewing gum loses its

flavor too quickly, may cause dental cavities, and is hard to dispose of. Think of solutions to these problems.

- *Decision trees.* Define the set of decisions that are to be made. For example, to develop a new grooming aid, decide on the user (men or women); type of aid (deodorant, shaving product, cologne); type of package (stick, bottle, spray); market (commercial, gift); and channel (vending machines, retailers, hotel rooms).
- *Brainstorming.* Gather a small group and pose a problem, such as, "Find new products and services that homes might need." Encourage freewheeling thinking, stimulate a maximum number of ideas, try new combinations, and avoid criticism at the beginning.
- *Synectics.* Pose a generic problem, such as how to open something, before posing the real one, hoping that it broadens the thinking.

A major source of ideas can come from futurists such as Alvin Toffler, John Naisbet, and Faith Popcorn and the trends they have spotted. Faith Popcorn became famous for her creative labeling of trends, including *anchoring* (religion, yoga), *being alive* (vegetarianism, meditation), *cashing out, clanning, cocooning, down-aging, fantasy adventure, 99 lives* (multitasking), *pleasure revenge, small indulgences,* and *vigilant consumers.* She would consult on how aligned a company's strategy is with these major trends, and often tell a company that it is off-trend in several ways.

Smart companies set up *idea markets.* They encourage their employees, suppliers, distributors, and dealers to offer suggestions that will save costs or yield new products, features, and services. They establish high-level committees that collect, evaluate, and choose the best ideas. And they reward those who suggest the best ideas. Alex Osborn, the developer of brainstorming, said: **"Creativity is so delicate a flower that praise tends to make it bloom, while discouragement often nips it in the bud."**

It is sad that creativity probably peaks at age 5 and then children go to school only to lose it. The educational emphasis on left brain cognitive learning tends to undernurture the creative right brain.

Customer Needs

Marketing's original mantra is to "find needs and fill them." The company finds needs by listening to or interviewing customers and then prepares an appropriate solution to each need. Today, however, there are few needs that companies don't know about or address. Pietro Guido, an Italian marketing consultant, wrote a book called *The No-Need Society* to make this point.

But there is another answer to the "no-need society"—that is, to create new needs. Sony's Akio Morita, in his *Made in Japan*, said: **"We don't serve markets. We create markets."** Consumers never thought of videotape recorders, video cameras, fax machines, Palms, and so on, until they were made.

Of course, new needs will emerge even if the old ones are satisfied. *Events* can create new needs. The tragedy of September 11, 2001, increased the need for greater security in the air, food supply, and transportation and the country rapidly responded with new security measures. *Trends* can create new needs, such as the interest in "Down-Aging." As people get older they want to feel and look younger, and this leads to buying sports cars, having plastic surgery, and using exercise equipment. So we can distinguish between existing needs and latent needs. Smart marketers will attempt to anticipate the next need and not only confine their attention to today's need.

Sometimes a need is obscured because a company has taken too limited a view of customers. Certain dogmas get set in concrete, such as the cosmetics industry dogma that women basically use cosmetics in order to be more attractive to men. Along came Anita Roddick, who started The Body Shop with the assumption that many women want products that will give good care to their skin. She added another value: that many women care about social issues and will patronize a company that cares.[19]

Greg Carpenter and Kent Nakamoto have challenged a core assumption of marketers that buyers initially know what they want.[20] Instead they *learn* what they want. And companies play a strong role in teaching buyers what to want. Different brand competitors add new features to their computers, cameras, and cellular phones that buyers may not have known of or asked for, and in the process, buyers form a better idea of what they want. Such companies are not just *market driven* (by customer needs), but are *market driving* (by innovation). In this sense, competition is less a race to meet consumer needs and more a race to define these needs.

One reason that early market entrants (such as Xerox or Palm) often gain sustained market leadership is because the attributes they initially build into their products define the wants that were otherwise ill-defined. Consumers see the attributes as defining the category. Late-entry competitors are forced to supply the same attributes at a minimum as well as innovate new ones.

Customer Orientation

How do you get your whole company to think and breathe customer? Jan Carlzon, former CEO of Scandinavian Airlines System (SAS), wrote *Moments of Truth*, in which he described how he got his whole workforce to focus on the customer.[21] He would emphasize at meetings that SAS handled 5 million customers a year and the average customer met about five SAS employees in connection with a single journey. This amounted to 25 million *moments of truth*, moments to deliver a positive brand experience to customers, whether delivered in person, over the phone, or by mail. Carlzon went further. He embarked on changing the company's structure, systems, and technology to empower the workforce to take any steps necessary to satisfy its target customers.

Today's CEOs must show employees, in financial terms, how much more affluent they and the firm would be if everyone focused on delivering great value to customers. The customers would spend more and cost the firm less to serve. Everyone would benefit, and special rewards would go to employees who rendered outstanding customer service.

The task begins with hiring the right people. You have to assess whether job candidates have not only the right skills but also the right attitudes. I was always struck by the fact that most people chose to fly Delta Air Lines from Chicago to Florida when they could have chosen

Eastern Airlines, which offered the same flight schedule. The difference: Delta hired its flight crews from the Deep South where friendliness is the norm; Eastern hired its flight crew from New York City.

Those whom you hire need good training. Disney runs a training program that lasts a week in order to convey what experience the company wants customers to have at Disneyland. A customer mind-set doesn't just happen. It has to be planned, implemented, and rewarded.

Yet companies tend to give two conflicting messages to their people. L. L. Bean and other companies train their people to value every customer: The customer comes first. Meanwhile they recognize that customers differ in their value to the company (i.e., what they add to revenue) and should therefore receive different levels of treatment.

American Airlines treats its customers differently beyond assigning different size seats and different cuisine. Passengers who have accumulated millions of miles get Executive Platinum Advantage treatment: they enter a shorter line at check-in, board earlier, get frequent upgrades, and receive surprise gifts such as interesting books and crystal Tiffany glassware.

The conclusion: Treat every customer with care but not necessarily equally.

To be truly customer-oriented, the firm should be run by *customer managers* (or customer group managers), not *brand managers*. They will find out the set of company products and services that their customers would care about and then work with the product and brand managers to deliver them.

Too many companies are *product driven* rather than *customer centered*. Their thinking goes like this:

Assets → Inputs → Offerings → Channels → Customers

Being product driven and heavily invested in assets, they push their offerings to every conceivable customer and fail to notice customer differences and values. Not knowing much about individual customers, they cannot efficiently *cross-sell* or *up-sell*. Both processes require capturing transaction and other information on individual customers and inferring what else they might be interested in. A customer-oriented company visualizes a different approach, called *sense-and-respond marketing*:

Customers → Channels → Offerings → Inputs → Assets

By starting with an understanding of customers, the company is in a much better position to develop appropriate channels, offerings, inputs, and assets.

Customer Relationship Management (CRM)

Everyone is talking about *customer relationship management (CRM)* as the new panacea. Yet it is an empty term until it is defined. Some people define it as the application of technology to learning more about each customer and being able to respond to them one-to-one. Others don't see it as a technology issue but rather a humane issue:

treating each customer with empathy and sensitivity. One cynic said that CRM is an expensive way to learn what otherwise might be learned by chatting with customers for five minutes.

Customer relationship marketing, in practice, involves the purchase of hardware and software that will enable a company to capture detailed information about individual customers that can be used for better target marketing. By examining a customer's past purchases, demographics, and psychographics, the company will know more about what the customer might be interested in. The company will send specific offers only to those with the highest possible interest and readiness to buy, and will save all the mailing or contact costs usually lost in mass marketing. Using the information carefully, the company can improve customer acquisition, cross-selling, and up-selling.

Yet CRM has not worked out that well in practice. Large companies sometimes spend $5 million to $10 million on CRM systems only to find disappointing results. Less than 30 percent of CRM-adopting companies report achieving the expected return from their CRM investments. And the problem isn't software failure (only 2 percent of the cases). *CRM-Forum* reported the following causes of failure: organizational change (29 percent), company politics/inertia (22 percent), lack of CRM understanding (20 percent), poor planning (12 percent), lack of CRM skills (6 percent), budget problems (4 percent), software problems (2 percent), bad advice (1 percent), other (4 percent).[23]

Too many companies see technology as a silver bullet that will help them overcome their bad habits. But adding new technology to an old company only makes it a more expensive old company. Companies should not invest in CRM until they reorganize to become customer-centric companies. Only then will they and their employees know how to use CRM properly.

Frederick Newell goes further and accuses CRM of falling far short of the answer to serving customers well.[24] CRM puts the company in the driver's seat with a hunting gun instead of putting the customer in the driver's seat with a hunting gun. He wants companies to *empower* customers, not *target* them. Instead of companies just sending mailings to sell their products (a product-centered approach), they need to ask their customers what they are interested in (and not interested in), what information they would like, what services they would want, and how, when, and how often they would accept communications from the company. Instead of relying on information about customers, companies can rely on information *from* customers. With this information, a company would be in a much better position to make meaningful offers to individual customers with much less waste of company money and customer time. Newell advocates replacing *customer relationship marketing (CRM)* with *customer management of relationships (CMR)*.

My belief is that the right kind of CRM or CMR is a positive development for companies and for society as a whole. It will humanize relationships. It will make the market work better. It will deliver better solutions to customers. (Also see Database Marketing.)

Customers

We now live in a customer economy where the customer is king. This is a result of production overcapacity. It is customers, not goods, that are in short supply.

Companies must learn how to move from a *product-making focus* to a *customer-owning focus*. Companies must wake up to the fact that they have a new boss—the customer. If your people are not thinking customer, they are not thinking. If they are not directly serving the customer, they'd better serve someone who is. If they don't take care of your customers, someone else will.

Companies must view the customer as a financial asset that needs to be managed and maximized like any other asset. Tom Peters sees customers as an "appreciating asset." They are the company's most important asset, and yet their value is not even found in the company's books.

Recognizing the value of this asset will hopefully lead companies to redesign their total marketing system toward capturing *customer share* and *customer lifetime value* through their products/services portfolio and branding strategies.

Over 30 years ago, Peter Drucker emphasized the importance of customer thinking to the success of a firm. He said that the purpose of a company is **"to create a customer. Therefore the business has two—and only two—basic functions: marketing and innovation. Marketing and innovation produce results: all the rest are costs."**[22]

L. L. Bean, the outdoor mail order firm, wholeheartedly practices a customer-oriented credo: **"A customer is the most important visitor on our premises. He is not dependent on us—we are dependent on him. He is not an outsider in our business—he is a part of it. We are not doing him a favor by serving him . . . he is doing us a favor by giving us the opportunity to do so."**

Products come and go. A company's challenge is to hold on to its customers longer than it holds on to its products. It needs to watch the *market life cycle* and the *customer life cycle* more than the *product life cycle*. Someone at Ford realized this: **"If we're not customer driven, our cars won't be either."**

Regrettably, companies spend most of their effort in acquiring new customers and not enough in retaining and growing business from their current customers. Companies spend as much as 70 percent of their marketing budget to attract new customers while 90 percent of their revenues come from current customers. Many companies lose money on their new customers during the first few years. By overfocusing on acquiring new customers and neglecting current customers, companies experience a customer attrition rate of between 10 and 30 percent a year. Then they waste further money on a never-ending effort to attract new customers or win back ex-customers to replace those they just lost.

Companies emphasize customer acquisition at the expense of customer retention in several ways. They set up compensation systems that reward getting new customers and do not reward salespeople as visibly for maintaining and growing existing accounts. Thus salespeople experience a thrill from winning a new account. Companies also act as if their current customers will stay on without special attention and service.

What should our aim be with customers? First, follow the Golden Rule of Marketing: *Market to your customers as you would want them to market to you.* Second, recognize that your success depends on your ability to make your customers successful. Aim to make your customers better off. Know their needs and exceed their expectations. Jack Welch, retired CEO of GE, put it this way: **"The best way to hold your customers is to constantly figure out how to give them more for less."** And remember, customers are increasingly buying on value, not on relationship alone.

It isn't enough to just satisfy your customers. Being satisfied is no longer satisfying. Companies always lose some satisfied customers. These customers switch to competitors who can satisfy them more. A company needs to deliver more satisfaction than its competitors.

Exceptional companies create delighted customers. They create *fans*. Take a lesson from Harley Davidson and the customer who said that he would rather give up smoking and other vices than be without a Harley.

Tom Monaghan, billionaire founder of Domino's Pizza, wants to make fans out of his customers. **"Whenever I see a new customer walk through the door, I see $10,000 burnt into their forehead."**

How do you know if you are doing a good job for the cus-

A German bank operated many branches throughout Germany. Each branch was deliberately kept small. Each branch manager had one task: to help clients increase their wealth. The branch manager did not simply take their deposits and make loans. The branch manager taught them how to save better, invest better, borrow better, and buy better. Each branch carried magazines on these subjects and offered free investment seminars to its customers, all to give them the skills to accumulate more wealth.

tomer? It is not shown in your profits this year but in your share of the customer's mind and heart. Companies that make steady gains in mind share and heart share will inevitably make gains in market share and profitability.

Marketing thinking is shifting from trying to maximize the company's profit from each transaction to maximizing the profit from each relationship. Marketing's future lies in *database marketing*, where we know enough about each customer to make relevant and timely offers customized and personalized to each customer. Instead of seeing a customer in every individual, we must see the individual in every customer.

But while it is important to serve all customers well, this does not mean that they must all be served equally well. All customers are important, but some are more important than others. Customers can be divided into those we enjoy, those we endure, and those we detest. But it is better to divide them into financial categories: platinum, gold, silver, iron, and lead customers. The better customers should be given more benefits, both to retain them longer and to give other customers an incentive to migrate upward.

One bank runs a club to which it invites only its high-asset depositors. Quarterly meetings are held, part social, part educational. The members hear from financial gurus, entertainers, and personalities. They would hate to lose their memberships by switching banks.

A company should classify its customers another way. The first group consists of the *Most Profitable Customers (MPCs)*, who deserve the most current attention. The second group are the *Most Growable Customers (MGCs)*, who deserve the most long-run attention. The third group are the *Most Vulnerable Customers (MVCs)*, who require early intervention to prevent their defection.

Not all customers, however, should be kept. There is a fourth category called *Most Troubling Customers (MTCs)*. Either they are unprofitable or the profits are too low to cover their nuisance value. Some should be "fired." But before firing them, give them a chance to reform. Raise their fees and/or reduce their service. If they stay, they are now profitable. If they leave, they will bleed your competitors.

Some customers are profitable but tough. They can be a blessing. If you can figure out how to satisfy your toughest customers, it will be easy to satisfy the rest.

Pay attention to customer complaints. Never underestimate the power of an irate customer to damage your reputation. Reputations are hard to build and easy to lose. IBM calls receiving complaints a joy. Customers who complain are the company's best friends. A complaint alerts the company to a problem that is probably losing customers and hopefully can be fixed.

Customer Satisfaction

Most companies pay more attention to their market share than to their customers' satisfaction. This is a mistake. Market share is a backward-looking metric; customer satisfaction is a forward-looking metric. If customer satisfaction starts slipping, then market share erosion will soon follow.

Companies need to monitor and improve the level of customer satisfaction. The higher the customer satisfaction, the higher the retention. Here are four facts:

1. Acquiring new customers can cost 5 to 10 times more than the costs involved in satisfying and retaining current customers.
2. The average company loses between 10 and 30 percent of its customers each year.
3. A 5 percent reduction in the customer defection rate can increase profits by 25 to 85 percent, depending on the industry.
4. The customer profit rate tends to increase over the life of the retained customer.[25]

One company bragged that 80 percent of its customers are satisfied or highly satisfied. This sounded pretty good until it learned that its leading competitor attained a 90 percent customer satisfaction score. The company was further dismayed to learn that this competitor was aiming for a 95 percent satisfaction score.

Companies that achieve a high satisfaction score should advertise it. J. D. Powers gave the Honda Accord the number one rating in customer satisfaction for several years, and this helped sell more Accords. Dell achieved the highest satisfaction ratings for its computer service and advertised this in its ads, giving prospects confidence that they could trust ordering a computer sight unseen from Dell.

The importance of aiming for high customer satisfaction is underscored in company ads. Honda says: **"One reason our customers are so satisfied is that we aren't."** Cigna advertises, **"We'll never be 100% satisfied until you are, too."** But don't make too big a claim. Holiday Inns ran a campaign a few years ago that promised "No Surprises." Guest complaints were so high that the slogan "No Surprises" was mocked, and Holiday Inn quickly canceled this slogan.

Customer satisfaction is a necessary but not sufficient goal. Customer satisfaction only weakly predicts customer retention in highly competitive markets. Companies regularly lose some percentage of their satisfied customers. Companies need to focus on customer retention. But even retention can be misleading, as when it is based on habit or an absence of alternative suppliers. A company needs to aim for a high level of customer loyalty or commitment. Loyal packaged-goods customers, for example, generally pay 7 percent to 10 percent more than nonloyal customers.

The company should therefore aim to delight customers, not simply satisfy them. Top companies aim to exceed customer expectations and leave a smile on customers' faces. But if they succeed, this becomes the norm. How can a company continue to exceed expectations after these expectations become very high? How many more surprises and delights can a company create? Interesting question!

Database Marketing

At the heart of CRM is database marketing. Your company needs to develop separate databases on customers, employees, products, services, suppliers, distributors, dealers, and retailers. The databases make it easier for marketers to develop relevant offerings for individual customers.

In building the customer database, you have to decide on what information to collect.

- The most important information to capture is the *transaction history* of each buyer. Knowing what a customer has purchased in the past affords many clues as to what he or she might be interested in buying next time.
- You could benefit by collecting *demographic* information about each buyer. For consumers, this means age, education, income, family size, and other attributes. For business buyers, this means job position, job responsibilities, job relationships, and contact addresses.
- You may want to add *psychographic* information describing the activities, interests, and opinions (AIO) of individual customers and how they think, make decisions, and influence others.

The second challenge is to get this information. You train your salespeople to gather and enter useful information into the customer's file after each sales visit. Your telemarketers can gather additional information by phoning customers or credit rating agencies.

The third challenge is to maintain and update the information. About 20 percent of the information in your customer database can become obsolete each year. You need telemarketers to phone a sample of customers each working day to update the information.

The fourth challenge is to use the information. Many companies fail to use the information they have. Supermarket chains have mountains of scanner data on individual customer purchases but fail to use these data for one-to-one marketing. Banks collect rich transaction information that mostly goes unanalyzed. At the very least, these companies need to hire a person skilled in *data mining*. By applying advanced statistical techniques, the data miner might detect interesting trends, segments, and opportunities.

With all these benefits, why don't more companies adopt database marketing? All this costs money. Consultant Martha Rogers of Peppers & Rogers Group does not deny the costs: **"Establishing a rich data warehouse can cost millions of dollars for the technology and the associated implementation and process changes. Throw in a few hundred thousand for strategic consulting, a little more for various data integration and change management issues, and voilà, you've got yourself one hefty investment."**[26]

Clearly one-to-one marketing is not for everyone. It is not for companies that sell a product purchased once in a lifetime, such as a grand piano. It is not for mass marketers like Wrigley to gather individual information about the millions of its gum-chewing customers. It is not for companies with small budgets, although the investment costs can be scaled down somewhat.

However, companies such as banks, telephone companies, business equipment firms, and many others normally collect lots of information on individual customers or dealers. The first company in each of these respective industries to exploit database marketing could achieve a substantial competitive lead.

There is a growing threat to effective database marketing that is coming from the inherent conflict between customer and company interests (see box).

What Customers Want

- We want companies not to have extensive personal information about us.
- We would be willing to tell some companies what we might like to be informed about.
- We would want companies to reach us only with relevant messages and media at proper times.
- We would want to be able to reach companies easily by phone or e-mail and get a quick response.

What Companies Want

- We want to know many things about each customer and prospect.
- We would like to tempt them with offers, including those that they might not have awareness of or initial interest in.
- We would like to reach them in the most cost-effective way regardless of their media preferences.
- We want to reduce the cost of talking with them live on the phone.

The irony is that as companies learn more about each customer in order to make more relevant offers, customers see this as an invasion of privacy. The matter is made worse by intrusive junk mail, junk phone calls, and junk e-mail. As privacy concerns rise and lead to legislation curtailing what companies may know about individual customers and how the companies can reach customers, companies will be forced to return to less efficient mass marketing and transaction-oriented marketing.

One answer is for companies to practice *permission marketing*, as promoted by Seth Godin.[27] You should ask your customers what information they will volunteer, what messages they would accept, and what contact media they would prefer.

Design

Design is a big idea, covering product design, service design, graphic design, and environmental design. Design provides a set of tools and concepts for preparing successful products and services. Yet too few managers know what design is or value it. At best, they equate design with style. Style is important, of course: We must accept that the Jaguar automobiles' success in the past was based on style. It certainly wasn't based on dependability, since most Jaguars had to be repaired frequently. An acquaintance of mine always owned two Jaguars, because one was usually in the repair shop.

Style, or appearance, does play a major role in many products: Apple's new computers, Bang & Olufsen's stereo equipment, Montblanc's writing instruments, Coca-Cola's famous bottle, and so on. Style can play a major role in differentiating your product from other products.

But design is a larger idea than how a product looks. A well-designed product, in addition to being attractive, would meet the following criteria:

- Easy to open the packaging.
- Easy to assemble.
- Easy to learn how to use.
- Easy to use.
- Easy to repair.
- Easy to dispose of.

Just consider "Easy to learn how to use." I recently purchased HP/Compaq's iPAQ, the personal digital assistant handheld computer. I couldn't remove a cellophane covering (not mentioned in the booklet) nor open the device's protective plastic cover nor figure out how to switch the cover to the other side. I couldn't figure out how to switch the data from my Palm handheld to my new iPAQ, something that most new buyers would want to do. After finally switching the data with the help of a friend, I encountered numerous screens that were hard to understand or perform operations on. The booklet, whose print could be read only under a microscope, was of no help. The whole product was a design fiasco, committed by engineers who thought they were selling it to engineers. I returned quietly to my beloved Palm and let the iPAQ languish.

This boils down to the fact that great design requires thinking through all of the customer's activities in acquiring, using, and disposing of the product. The most basic thing is to know who the target customer is. I remember a company that designed a floor-cleaning machine to be used after hours to clean offices. The machine looked great and had nice features. But the machine didn't sell. The machine could easily be pushed by the average man but was too heavy to be pushed by most women. It turned out that many of the users would be women, and this had been overlooked by the designers.

Toyota is smarter about defining the customer and thinking like the customer. In designing new doors for a car targeted largely toward women, Toyota engineers put on long fingernails to see how this would affect opening and closing the doors.

Some companies—Gillette, Apple, Sony, Bang & Olufsen—have appointed a high-level vice president of design to add value to every product their companies create. By establishing this position, they are announcing to everyone the importance of design to the success of their products.

Design applies to service businesses as well as products. Walk into Starbucks for coffee and you will appreciate the role of environmental design. Dark wood counters, bright colors, fine textures. Walk into a Ritz-Carlton hotel and appreciate the lobby's regal quality.

Differentiation

The stock market is a perfect example of an undifferentiated market. If you want to buy 100 shares of IBM, you will buy it at the lowest price. There may be 1,000 people ready to sell shares of IBM. All you care about is who will charge the least. No characteristic of the seller—how long he/she has held the shares, whether he/she cheats on income tax or spouse, what his/her religion is—matters to you.

We say that a product market resembles a commodity market when we don't care whose product or brand we take ("They are all the same") or we don't need to know anything about the seller. Thus we would say that oranges in a supermarket amount to a commodity if they all look alike and we don't care to know the grower or the orchard.

But there are three things that could violate the assumption of an undifferentiated market.

- First, the products may look different. In the case of oranges, they may come in different sizes, shapes, colors, and tastes, and with different prices. We can call this *physical differentiation*.
- Second, the products may bear different brand names. We call this *brand differentiation*. Oranges carry brand names such as Sunkist or Florida's Best.

- Third, the customer may have developed a satisfying relationship with one of the suppliers. We call this *relationship differentiation*. For example, although the brands are well known, one company may have provided better and faster answers to the customer's questions.

Harvard's Theodore Levitt threw down the gauntlet when he said: **"There is no such thing as a commodity. All goods and services are differentiable."**[28] He saw commodities as simply products waiting for a redefinition. Frank Perdue, who produces one of the most popular brands of chicken, would boast: **"If you can differentiate a dead chicken, you can differentiate anything."** No wonder one professor tells his MBA class that any student who uses the word "commodity" during a case discussion would be fined $1.

Yet some companies believe they can win through pure will power. Some years ago, the runner-up razor blade manufacturer in Brazil challenged Gillette, the market leader. We asked the challenger if his company offered the consumer a better razor blade. "No" was the reply. "A lower price?" "No." "A better package?" "No." "A clever advertising campaign?" "No." "Better allowances to the trade?" "No." "Then how do you expect to take share away from Gillette?" "Sheer determination" was the reply. Needless to say, the offensive failed.

Tom Peters broadcasts the mantra: **"Be distinct or extinct."** But not every difference is distinctive. Establish "meaningful differences, not better sameness."

Differentiation can be achieved in many ways (see box).

Jack Trout's book, *Differentiate or Die*, shows dozens of ways companies have managed to produce a differentiated product, service, experience, or image in the minds of customers.[29]

Greg Carpenter, Rashi Glazer, and Kent Nakamoto, don't even hold that the differentiation needs to be meaningful.[30] For some products, such as detergents, all the valuable attributes may have al-

How to Differentiate

- *Product* (features, performance, conformance, durability, reliability, repairability, style, design).
- *Service* (delivery, installation, customer training, consulting, repair).
- *Personnel* (competence, courtesy, credibility, reliability, responsiveness, communication skill).
- *Image* (symbols, written and audio/video media, atmosphere, events).

ready been discovered and exploited. They argue that "meaningless differentiation" can work. For example, Alberto Culver makes a shampoo called Natural Silk to which it does add silk, despite admitting in an interview that silk does nothing for hair. But this kind of attribute attracts attention, creates a distinction, and implies a better working formula.

# Direct Mail

When direct mail is at its worst, it consists of a cold mailing to a list of names and addresses with the hope of hitting a 1 to 2 percent response. The response is low because the message doesn't go to people with a need for the product or arrive at the time they need it. Hence the term "junk mail."

When direct mail is refined, the company segments the list, finds the best prospects, and limits the mailing to them. In this way, the company saves money with a smaller mailing and achieves a higher response rate.

Most mailings focus on achieving a single sale. They lack anything related to building a customer relationship and an emotional bond.

The best case is where the company's offers satisfy the customers and where the company mails neither too frequently nor too infrequently and becomes a respected supplier of a certain set of satisfying products and services.

What I can't understand is why I receive the same catalogs over and over even though I never buy anything. Don't they notice this? Why don't they send an e-mail asking whether I want to continue receiving their catalog? This is the essence of permission marketing, and it would save these catalog companies a lot of money.

Distribution and Channels

For many companies, making the product doesn't cost as much as bringing it to the market! Farmers know this well when they see how small a percentage of the final retail price they receive for their crops. Marketing in many cases now averages 50 percent of total company costs. Producers would like to eliminate the middleman, whom they see as charging too much. But while you can eliminate the middleman, you cannot eliminate the functions he performs. You and/or the customer would have to perform the same functions and probably wouldn't do them as well.

How can a company bring its new products into the market? Every company has to figure out a *go-to-market strategy*. In simpler times, the company would hire salespeople to sell to distributors, wholesalers, retailers, or directly to final users. Today the number of go-to-market alternatives has exploded:

Field sales reps	Intranet
Strategic allies	Extranet
Business partners	Web sites
Master or local distributors	E-mail
Integrators	Business-to-business exchanges
Value-added resellers	Auctions

53

Manufacturers' agents   Fax machines
Brokers   Direct mail
Franchises   Newspapers
Telemarketers   Television
Telesales agents

No wonder Peter Drucker said: **"The greatest change will be in distribution channels, not in new methods of production or consumption."** Choosing the right channels, convincing them to carry your merchandise, and getting them to work as partners is a major challenge. Too many companies see themselves as selling to distributors, instead of selling *through* them.

How many marketing channels should a company use to distribute its products and services? The higher the number of channels, the greater the company's *market coverage* and rate of growth of its sales. This principle is well illustrated by Starbucks Coffee Company. Starbucks started with only one channel, namely company-owned stores that were staffed carefully and operated profitably. Later Starbucks franchised operations in other venues: airports, bookstores, and college campuses. The company recently signed a licensing agreement with Albertson's food chain to open coffee bars in its supermarkets. Not only is Starbucks coffee served in these venues, but other Starbucks products are sold along with coffee. A comedian quipped about Starbucks: "I don't know how fast they are growing but they just opened one in my living room." Adding more channels creates rapid growth.

But at least two problems can arise in adding new market channels. First, product or service quality may suffer because the company gained market coverage at the expense of *market control*. Does Starbucks coffee served on a United Air Lines flight taste as good as a cup made and served in a Starbucks store? Do all vendors remember to dispose of Starbucks coffee if it isn't sold within two hours? Secondly, the company may encounter growing problems of *channel conflict.* Some Starbucks outlets may complain that the company franchised nearby outlets to also sell Starbucks coffee, thus hurting their sales. Or that some outlets are charging less for Starbucks coffee than other outlets. In both cases, Starbucks would have gained increased market coverage but lost some market control.

The alternative is to stick to one channel and develop it with very tight controls. For example, the Rolex Watch Company could easily place its famous watches in many more outlets. Instead it restricts its coverage to only high-end jewelers who are spaced geographically and who agree to carry a certain level of inventory, use certain display patterns, and place specific levels of annual local advertising. Rolex thus has achieved high market control and does not face poor service problems or channel conflict problems. But its market growth is slower.

Whatever the number of market channels a company uses, it must integrate them to achieve an efficient supply system. Most companies rely on a high percentage of their business results coming from their channel partners. They need to systematize *partner relationship management (PRM)* through adopting PRM software. The software can improve the information flow and reduce the cost of communication, ordering, transactions, and payment.

Manufacturers who use distributors to reach retailers give up some control of the retailers and the final customers. Yet if the manufacturer sold direct to either the retailers or the final customers, it would have to carry on the same channel functions of selling, financing, information gathering, servicing, risk taking, transportation, and storage. If distributors can do this better and add value, then the distributor channel is justified. The key point is that all the channel functions must be performed and allocated efficiently among the channel partners.

A company operating multiple channels must operate them with similar policies. A bookstore chain such as Borders must have its brick-and-mortar stores be prepared to also accept returned books purchased from Borders online. Nor can Borders charge lower prices online without hurting its store sales.

Here are two excellent examples of integrated channels:

- Charles Schwab, the financial powerhouse, delivers an excellent branded experience to its customers whether reached online, over the telephone, or in its walk-in branches.
- Hewlett-Packard (HP) has an excellent web site where customers can find information about any HP product or service. Customers can place an order online or by phoning Hewlett-Packard. They will receive postsale support by contacting HP and being directed to the nearest local business partner.

Another option is to set up special channels for favored customers. Many banks provide private banking channels to customers with large deposits. Dell provides a separate extranet for each high-value business customer. Schwab's premier customers are assigned to a dedicated account team that can always be reached through a toll-free phone number.

Your company must not only develop and operate efficient marketing channels but be prepared to add new ones and drop failing ones. Distribution channels are dynamic. They can create a competitive advantage when used right, but become a competitive liability when used poorly.

Employees

Your employees are your business! They can make or break your marketing plans. Hal Rosenbluth, owner of a major travel agency, stunned the marketing world with the title of his book, *The Customer Comes Second*.[31] Then who comes first? Employees, he said. His point is particularly applicable to service businesses. Service businesses involve intensive people contact. If the hotel clerk is sullen, if the waitress is bored, if the accountant doesn't return phone calls, then clients will take their business elsewhere. So companies like Rosenbluth Travel, Marriott, and British Airways operate on the following formula: First train the employees to be friendly, knowledgeable, and reliable; this will lead to satisfied customers who will return again; and this will create a growing profit stream for the shareholders.

Anita Roddick, who founded The Body Shop, agrees: **"Our people [employees] are my first line of customers."** By viewing her employees as customers, she aims to understand and meet their needs. Walt Disney held the same view: **"You'll never have great customer relations till you have good employee relations."** The way your employees feel is ultimately the way your customers are going to feel.

Some companies go to great lengths to find the right employees. There isn't a people shortage so much as a talent shortage. The people that you hire today create your future tomorrow. Using a tight definition of the personality and character traits that it seeks in employees, Southwest Airlines hires only 4 percent of its 90,000 applicants each year. Then it makes sure to give them a career, not just a job.

A company that pays little to its employees will get back little in return. If you pay your people in peanuts, you will get monkeys. It will cost you lots of money to replace employees who leave. Finding talented and motivated employees and retaining them is a key to business success.

Smart companies pay generously. They attract the best people who outperform average people by a higher multiple than the higher pay. They experience less employee turnover and lower costs of hiring (because people flock to this company) and of training (because they hire people with more capabilities).

Pay is only part of the answer to good employee management. Companies are human and social organizations, not just economic machines. Employees need to feel that they belong to a worthwhile organization doing worthwhile work and making a worthwhile contribution. Gary Hamel said, **"Create a cause, not a business."**

Companies must prepare a compelling *value proposition* not only for their customers but also for their employees. The aim of *internal marketing* is to treat the employees as a customer group. Great organizations give even the lowest workers a good feeling. Consider the following:

- Bill Pollard, retired chairman of ServiceMaster, had a credo that included "We should treat everybody with dignity and worth." At a board meeting, coffee was accidentally spilled on the carpet and a janitor was called in. Bill took the cleaning solvent from the janitor and knelt down to clean the carpet himself to spare the janitor from having to do so in front of all the board members. **"You get respect by giving it."** (Sara Lawrence-Lightfoot, Harvard Graduate School of Education)

• One day a vice president said to Herb Kelleher, then CEO of Southwest Airlines, "It is harder for me to see you than [it is for] a ticket handler at our company." "Yes," said Herb. "The reason is that he is more important." Herb Kelleher went on to rename the Personnel Department the People Department. He also renamed the Marketing Department the Customer Department.

A company's people can be the strongest source of competitive advantage. John Thompson of Heidrick & Struggles advises: **"Get fewer, smarter people to deliver more value to customers faster."** Jeff Bezos of Amazon says: **"We look for people who have a natural inclination to be intensely focused on the customer."**

Companies need to inculcate their brand values into their employees. Intel wants to inculcate "risk-taking," Disney "creativity," 3M "innovativeness." Some companies include in the employee's remuneration a certain percentage for company values performance. General Electric links 50 percent of its incentive remuneration to value performance. Cisco bases 20 percent of bonuses on the employees' customer satisfaction scores. A company should go further and honor outstanding employee performance through recognition programs, newletters, CEO awards, and the like. John Kotter and Jim Heskett, in *Corporate Culture and Performance*,[32] empirically demonstrated that companies with strong cultures based on shared values far outperform companies with weak cultures by a huge margin.

A company must make sure that its employees understand that they are not working for the company. They are working for the customer. Jack Welch of GE would repeatedly tell his employees: **"Nobody can guarantee your job. Only customers can guarantee your job."** Sam Walton of Wal-Mart echoed the same sentiment: **"The customer is the only one who can fire us all."** Larry Bossidy, chairman of Honeywell International, Inc., sent out the same message: **"It's not management who decides how many people are on the payroll.**

It's customers." Some companies include a note in the employee's paycheck envelope: "This check is brought to you by the customer."

Sam Walton of Wal-Mart required the following employee pledge: **"I solemnly swear and declare that every customer that comes within 10 feet of me, I will smile, look them in the eye, and greet them, so help me Sam."** Lands End instructs its employees: **"Don't worry about what's good for the Company—worry about what's good for the Customer."** (See Innovation.)

Entrepreneurship

Businesses begin with an idea in the head of an entrepreneur. The entrepreneur is filled with passion and energy to create something new. The entrepreneur is the modern equivalent of pioneers searching for new frontiers. Entrepreneurs take risks against high odds. Their goal is not making money so much as making something new. And when they succeed, they create jobs and incomes for more people.

But according to a Chinese saying: "To open a business is very easy; to keep it open is very difficult." And the hours are long. **"Being in your own business is working 80 hours a week so that you can avoid working 40 hours a week for someone else."** (Ramona E. F. Arnett)

If the entrepreneur succeeds, the business grows. Comfort takes over and routine sets in. The business focuses on operations and efficiency and becomes a well-oiled machine. What is lost is the entrepreneurial passion. The big danger is that the firm's products and services may become increasingly irrelevant in a changing marketplace. The big need is to keep a spirit of entrepreneurship alive.

Your company can nurture an intrapreneurial spirit in a number of ways. Encourage ideas. Reward good ideas. Set up a collection system for new ideas. Set up a skunk works. Every 90 days gather all the employees at an "idea bragging session," where employees describe how they got their new ideas.

xperiential Marketing

We talk about marketing *goods* and *services*, but Joe Pine and James Gilmore think that we should be talking about marketing *experiences*[33]—or designing experiences around our goods and services. The idea has many sources. Great restaurants are known for their experience as much as their food. Starbucks charges us $2 or more to experience coffee at its finest. A restaurant such as Planet Hollywood and Hard Rock Café is specifically set up as an experience. Las Vegas hotels, anxious to distinguish themselves, take on the character of ancient Rome or New York City. But the master is Walt Disney, who created the opportunity to experience the cowboy West, fairyland castles, pirate ships, and the like. The aim of the experiential marketer is to add drama and entertainment to what otherwise might pass as stale fare.

Thus we enter Niketown to buy basketball shoes and confront a 15-foot photo of Michael Jordan. We then proceed to the basketball court to see whether the shoes help us score better. Or we enter REI, an outdoor equipment chain store, and test out climbing equipment on the store's climbing wall, or test out a rainproof coat by going under a simulated rainfall. Or we enter Bass Pro to buy a fishing rod and test it by casting in the store's pool of fish.

All merchants offer services; your challenge is to escort your customer through a memorable experience.

inancial Marketing

I have always urged marketers to be strong in financial thinking. This is not a natural inclination of marketers. They are marketers because they are more interested in people than in numbers.

Yet few marketers will rise to the top of an organization unless they have a good grasp of financial thinking. They need to understand income statements, cash flow statements, balance sheets, and budgets. Concepts such as asset turnover, return on investment (ROI), return on assets (ROA), free cash flow, economic value added

(EVA), market capitalization, and cost of capital must be as familiar to them as sales, market share, and gross margins.

Companies today are focusing on shareholder value. The CEO is not satisfied when the marketing vice president shows that the recent marketing initiatives have resulted in increased customer awareness, knowledge, satisfaction, or retention. The CEO wants to know marketing's impact on ROI and stock prices. Clearly marketers must start linking their marketing metrics to financial metrics.

Corporate cost cutters are now carefully scrutinizing marketing-related costs. Marketers must now justify every item in their marketing budgets and be able to show how each contributes to shareholder value.

One useful step is for companies to appoint *marketing controllers*. These are skilled financial people who understand the marketing process and what it takes to win. They know that advertising, sales promotion, and other marketing initiatives are necessary. Their task is to make sure that the money is spent well.

You can improve marketing's financial returns in two basic ways:

- Increase your *marketing efficiency*. Marketing efficiency involves reducing the costs of activities that the company must carry out. Suppose the company needs point-of-purchase displays and goes to only one display firm and orders them. Had the company invited competitive bids, it might have found a lower price for the same or better quality. Or a company might perform its own marketing research for X dollars, only to find that equivalent or even better quality research might have been outsourced to a marketing research firm for fewer dollars. Other examples: hunting down excessive communication and transportation expenses, closing unproductive sales offices, cutting back on unproven promotional programs and tactics, and putting advertising agencies on a pay-for-performance basis.

- Increase your *marketing effectiveness*. Marketing effectiveness represents the company's search for a more productive marketing mix. A company might increase its marketing effectiveness by replacing higher cost channels with lower cost channels, shifting advertising money into public relations, adding or subtracting product features, or adopting technology that improves the company's information and communication effectiveness.

The aim of marketing is to maximize not just your sales but your long-term profits. While salespeople focus on sales, marketers must focus on profits. Show me a top marketer, and you will be showing me a person who is financially well-versed.

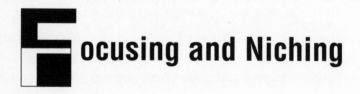

Focusing and Niching

Wise companies focus. An old saying is that if you chase two monkeys, both will escape.

The mass market is made up of many niches. The problem of being a mass marketer is that you will attract nichers who will take better aim at specific customer groups and meet their needs better. As these groups are pulled away, the mass marketer's market shrinks.

Your choice therefore is whether to be a "gorilla" or a "guerrilla."—to be niched or be a nicher. I would argue that there are riches in niches. The customers in a niche are happy that someone is paying attention to their needs. And if your company serves them well, you will own the niche. Although the volume is low in a niche, the margin is high. Competitors will keep out because the niche is too small to support two players.

What does a successful nicher do for a second act? What the nicher should not do is become a generalist and go after the mass market. There are three sound strategies:

1. *Sell more products and services to the same niche.* USAA, the giant insurance company, originally sold only auto insurance to military officers. Then it added life insurance, credit cards, mutual funds, and other financial products to sell to military officers.

2. *Look for latent or adjacent members in the niche.* USAA recognized that it would eventually run out of enough military officers to sell to. So it decided to extend its target market to include all members of the military.

3. *Look for additional niches.* Every niche is vulnerable to attack or decay. The best defense against the vulnerability of a single niche is to own two or more niches. In this way, the company not only enjoys a high margin from its good service to the niche, but it also enjoys high volume through owning a portfolio of niches. A good example is Johnson & Johnson, which aside from being a strong force in a few mass consumer markets, is the technical or market leader in hundreds of specialized business-to-business markets.

Nichers are not necessarily small companies. Professor Hermann Simon, in his *Hidden Champions*,[34] lists scores of midsize German companies that enjoy over 50 percent market shares in well-defined global niches. Examples include Steiner Optical with 80 percent of the world's military field glasses market; Tetra Food making 80 percent of the food for feeding tropical fish; and Becher producing 50 percent of the world's oversized umbrellas. These and other companies pursue well-defined niches in the global marketplace, and although they are less visible to the public, they are highly profitable.

orecasting and the Future

The company that doesn't see trouble ahead is headed for real trouble. That's why it hires economists, consultants, and futurists.

Yet people must be cautious about predicting the future. Ben Franklin said, **"It is easy to see; hard to foresee."** An old saying is that those who live by the crystal ball will eat ground glass.

So many eminent observers have made wildly erroneous predictions.

- Thomas Edison opined that "the phonograph is of no commercial value."
- Irving Fisher, eminent Yale economics professor, said in September 1929, just before the Wall Street crash, "Stock prices have reached what looks like a permanently high plateau."

- Thomas J. Watson of IBM said in 1947: "I think there is a world market for about five computers."
- Ken Olson, former CEO of Digital Equipment Corporation, said in 1977, "There is no reason for any individual to have a computer in their home."
- Jack Welch, the retired chairman of GE, admitted to three forecasting errors during his career. When U.S. inflation was running at 20 percent, he forecasted that inflation would remain in the double digits. When oil hit $35 a barrel, he predicted that oil's price would rise to $100. When Japan was in its prime, he predicted that the Japanese would continue to take over more American industries.

All of these show the weakness of using today's situation to predict tomorrow's situation. The story is told about an auto company that increased its production of green cars after noticing a spike in their sales. The company didn't realize that dealers were slashing prices to get rid of green cars.

John R. Pierce of Bell Labs beautifully explained why so many predictions fail: **"The trouble with the future is that there are so many of them."**

The inimitable Yogi Berra said that **"prediction is very hard, especially of the future."** He also despaired: **"The future ain't what it used to be."**

The most truthful prediction is that business will be either better or worse. The same can be said for the economy.

Woody Allen commented on how to handle bad times: **"More than anytime in history, mankind faces a crossroads. One path leads to despair and utter hopelessness, the other to total extinction. Let us pray that we have the wisdom to choose correctly."**

Businesses have relied on economists to predict the future. There are two types of economists: those who can't predict the future and know it, and those who can't predict the future and don't know it. After asking different economists for an opinion, Harry Truman finally gave up and requested a one-handed economist. He did not want to hear the words: "On the other hand." Basically, economists exist to make astrologers look good.

In spite of this, in order to be in front your business needs to forecast where customers and the economy are moving. Wayne Gretzky, the brilliant hockey star, when asked how he is always in the right position, said: **"It isn't where the puck is; it's where the puck will be."**

Yet watch out for experts who give a forecast in the form of a number or a date, but not both.

The truth is that the future is already here; it has already happened. The task is to find and study what the small percentage of future-defining customers want. The future is already here but is unevenly distributed in different companies, industries, and countries.

Dennis Gabor, the business strategist, is less concerned with predicting the future. He believes: **"The best way to predict the future is to invent it."** Your company faces an infinite number of futures and must decide on which one it wants.

Goals and Objectives

The most generic goal of business is to earn more than the cost of capital. The goal is to make today's investment worth more tomorrow. If this happens, the company has achieved economic value added (EVA).

Companies may add other goals, but they must be thought through carefully:

- *Corporate growth.* Companies need to grow, but it must be profitable growth. Too many companies go on acquisition binges or geographical expansions only to grow their top lines at a terrible cost to their bottom lines. They are buying growth rather than earning it.
- *Market share.* Too many companies aim to collect as many customers as possible. But more market share often means picking up more unreliable customers. These companies would be smarter to focus on nurturing loyal customers, getting to know them better, and finding more goods and services they may need or want.
- *Return on sales.* Some companies focus on achieving or maintaining a certain margin. But the margin is meaningless without matching it to the sales volume generated per dollar of assets (asset turnover).
- *Earnings per share growth.* Companies set targets for their earnings per share (EPS). But EPS does not necessarily reflect the return on capital because companies can raise EPS by buying back shares, writing off certain costs, and employing various creative accounting measures.
- *Reputation.* Companies should strive for a good reputation. A company's main reputational goals should be fourfold: to be (1) the supplier of choice to customers, (2) the employer of choice to employees, (3) the partner of choice to distributors, and (4) the company of choice to investors. Its reputational capital will contribute to its primary goal, earning a higher return than the cost of capital.

After a company clarifies its goal(s), it needs to develop specific objectives for the corporate level, the business divisions, and the various departments. These objectives drive the planning process and carry incentives and rewards. Peter Drucker, who fathered the idea of *management by objectives*, nevertheless lamented: **"Management by objectives works if you know the objectives. Ninety percent of the time you don't."**

Yogi Berra, the colorful New York Yankees catcher, warned: **"If you don't know where you're going, you're liable to end up someplace else."** But then how do you set an objective? His answer didn't help: **"When you come to a fork in the road, take it."**

Think carefully about your goals and objectives. For example, speed is useful only if you are running in the right direction. A pilot got on the intercom and said: "I've got good news and bad news. The bad news first: I don't know where we're going. The good news: We're getting there fast."

Growth Strategies

It is not enough to be profitable. Companies must also grow. In fact, if you don't grow, you won't be profitable for long. Staying with the same customers, products, and markets is a recipe for disaster.

Investors want to see a growing top line; employees want to

have more advancement opportunities; and distributors want to serve a growing company. Growth is energizing. An old maxim says: "If you stand still, you get shot."

Companies often excuse their lack of growth by saying that they are in a mature market. All they are expressing is a lack of imagination. Larry Bossidy, CEO of Honeywell, observed: **"There's no such thing as a mature market. We need mature executives who can find ways to grow. . . . Growth is a mind-set."** If the car market was mature, how come the minivan sent Chrysler into a growth spurt? If the steel industry is mature, how do we explain Nucor? If Sears thought that there was no growth in retailing, how do we explain Wal-Mart or Home Depot?

Companies have tried several paths to growth: *cost and price cutting, aggressive price increases, international expansion, acquisition,* and *new products.* Each has problems. Price cuts are usually matched and neutralized. Price increases are difficult to pass on during sluggish economic times. Most international markets are now highly competitive or protected. Company acquisitions are expensive and have not proven very profitable. And the numbers of new product winners are few.

What companies fail to realize is that their markets are rarely fully penetrated. *All markets consist of segments and niches.* American Express recognized this and created the Corporate Card, the Gold Card, and the Platinum Card. To grow, a company can make four segment moves:

1. *Move into adjacent segments.* Nike's first success was making superior running shoes for serious runners. Later it moved into shoes for basketball, tennis, and football. Still later, it moved into aerobic shoes.
2. *Do a finer segmentation.* Nike found that it could segment the basketball shoe market into finer segments: shoes for the aggressive player, the high-jumping player, and so on.

3. *Skip into new segments (categories).* Nike moved into selling clothing tied to the various sports.
4. *Resegment the whole market.* Nike's competitor, Reebok, re-segmented the market by introducing stylish shoes for the leisure market that could be worn every day without a sport in mind.

Another growth approach is to redefine the market in which your company operates. GE's Jack Welch told his people: **"Redefine your market to one in which your current share is no more than 10 percent."** Instead of thinking that your company has a 50 percent market share, it should see itself as operating in a larger market where it enjoys less than 10 percent of that market. Here are some examples:

- Nike now defines itself as being in the sports market rather than the shoe and clothing market. It is considering selling sports equipment and even offering services such as managing athletes' careers.
- The late Roberto Goizueta told his company, Coca-Cola, that while Coca-Cola had a 35 percent share of the soft drink market, it had only a 3 percent share of the total beverage market and it needed to increase its share.
- Armstrong World Industries, Inc., moved from floor coverings to ceilings to total interior surface decoration.
- Citicorp thought that it had a substantial share of the banking market but realized that it had only a small share of the total financial market, which includes much more than banking.
- AT&T stopped thinking of itself as a long distance telephone company and moved into carrying voice, image, text, and data on telephone lines, cable, cellular phones, and the Internet.
- Taco Bell went from an in-store fast-food restaurant to "feeding people everywhere," including kiosks, convenience stores, airports, and high schools.

Management can search for growth opportunities using the following framework:

- *Sell more of the current products to the current customers.* Encourage customers to consume more per occasion or consume on more occasions.
- *Sell additional products to the current customers.* Identify other products that the current customers might need.
- *Sell more of the current products to new customers.* Introduce your current products into new geographical areas or into new market segments.
- *Sell new products to new customers.* Acquire or build new businesses that cater to new markets.

Achieving growth requires developing a growth mentality in the company's personnel and partners. Watch for needs not being currently satisfied. Instead of starting from the company's current products and competencies (inside-out thinking), seek growth by sensing the untapped needs of existing and new customers (outside-in thinking). Look at the end users' needs, then your immediate customers' needs, and finally decide which needs you can meet profitably.

Adrian Slywotzky and Richard Wise proposed that companies have "hidden assets" that they could apply to satisfying "higher order" needs in their markets. "Most executives have spent years learning to create growth using products, factories, facilities, and working capital. They have spent much less time thinking about how to use a combination of relationships, market position, networks, and information—their hidden assets—to create value for customers and growth for investors."[35]

Guarantees

Guarantees are getting more fashionable. Guarantees can be powerful builders of corporate value and credibility. They may promise money back, compensation, or product replacement. But they must be relevant, unconditional, believable, and easy to understand. Ignore those who promise to help you use 30 pounds in a week, speak French in a day, or cure baldness.

Here are companies whose powerful guarantees have created strong followings:

- *Hampton Inn* guarantees that its rooms will give "complete satisfaction or your night's stay is free."
- *Loblaws* (Canada) offers to replace its private-label food items with national brands if customers don't consider Loblaws a better value.
- *Xerox* will replace any Xerox product within three years until the customer is fully satisfied.
- A. T. Cross will replace its pens and pencils for life. The customer mails the broken pen or pencil to the company and it is repaired or replaced free and mailed back.

- *Saturn* will take its new car back within 30 days if the customer is not satisfied.
- *Allied Van Lines* will pay $100 for each day of delay in moving a customer's goods.
- *BBBK Pest Control* will refund customer money if it fails to eradicate all pests and will pay for the next exterminator.

Here is how L. L. Bean words its well-known guarantee: **"All of our products are guaranteed to give 100% satisfaction in every way. Return anything purchased from us at any time if it proves otherwise. We will replace it, refund your purchase price or credit your credit card, as you wish. We do not want you to have anything from L. L. Bean that is not completely satisfactory."**

There are always some companies, however, that are more ready to proclaim guarantees than to honor them. Their lawyers word the guarantees with hidden conditions and special requirements that make them into nonguarantees. But in the process, the company creates a growing band of angry people bent on discrediting the company to whoever will listen.

Image and
Emotional Marketing

Companies are increasingly turning to image and emotional marketing to win customer mind share and heart share. Although this has gone on from the beginning of time, today it is accelerating. The old marketing mantra advised companies to outperform competitors on some benefit and to promote this benefit: "Volvo is the safest car"; "Tide cleans better than any other detergent"; "Wal-Mart sells at the lowest prices." Going under the name of *benefit marketing*, it assumed that consumers were more influenced by rational arguments than by emotional appeals. But in today's economy, companies rapidly copy any competitor's advantage until it no longer remains. Volvo's benefit of making the safest car means less when customers start seeing most cars as safe.

More companies are now trying to develop images that move the heart instead of the head. Those addressed to the head tend to state the same benefits. So companies are trying to sell an attitude like Nike's "Just do it." Celebrities are shown wearing "milk mustaches." Prudential wants people to have a "piece of the rock." These campaigns work more on affect than cognition.

Companies are turning to anthropologists and psychologists to develop messages that touch emotions more deeply. One approach is to build the image of the product around some deep archetype—the hero, antihero, siren, wise old man—that resides in the collective unconscious.

You can readily find out how your customers and noncustomers see your company and your competitors. A marketing research firm would ask: "How old a person is this company?" (The answer may be a "teenager" in the case of Apple Computer and a "grandfather" in the case of IBM.) Or "What animal does this company remind you of?" (Hope for a lion or a monkey, not an elephant or a dinosaur.)

Implementation and Control

There is a constant debate about whether strategy or execution is more important. Peter Drucker observed that **"a plan is nothing unless it degenerates into work."** Yet a poor plan with great implementation is no better than a good plan with poor implementation. The truth is that both are necessary for success.

Implementation snafus are legion. Kodak's ads for a new camera drew people into stores only to find that the cameras hadn't arrived.

A major bank announced a new savings plan in the newspapers but hadn't explained the plan to its branch managers. An engineering firm made a decision to sell its services in the Middle East but could not find any capable person who spoke Arabic and would be willing to transfer there. A hotel decided to make service its major value proposition but let service be run by a weak manager with a small budget and an insufficient staff.

Good implementation needs buy-in from those who are to carry out the plan. The best way to get their buy-in is to have them participate in the plan's development. Thus salespeople are more likely to accept the marketing plan if a sales representative participated in its development and if the target volumes and prices are plausible. So the planner's first need is to sell the plan inside, not outside.

Control is the way that we catch failures in implementation or strategy. The company may have implemented poorly, set the wrong marketing mix, aimed at the wrong target market, or done poor initial research. Control is not a singular thing but a host of tools for making sure that the company is on track. The tools fall under four types of control shown here.[36]

Types of Marketing Control

Type of Control	Prime Responsibility	Purpose of Control	Approach
I. Annual-plan control	Top management; middle management	To examine whether the planned results are being achieved	• Sales analysis • Market-share analysis • Sales-to-expense ratios • Financial analysis • Market-based scorecard analysis

Type of Control	Prime Responsibility	Purpose of Control	Approach
II. Profitability control	Marketing controller	To examine where the company is making and losing money	Profitability by: • Product • Territory • Customer • Segment • Trade channel • Order size
III. Efficiency control	Line and staff management; marketing controller	To evaluate and improve the spending efficiency and impact of marketing expenditures	Efficiency of: • Sales force • Advertising • Sales promotion • Distribution
IV. Strategic control	Top management; marketing auditor	To examine whether the company is pursuing its best opportunities with respect to markets, products, and channels	• Marketing effectiveness rating instrument • Marketing audit • Marketing excellence review • Company ethical and social responsibility review

The processes of planning, implementation, and control constitute a virtuous feed forward/feed back system. If your company is not achieving its goals, either you are implementing your plan poorly or your plan has become irrelevant and needs fixing.

Information and Analytics

A former CEO of Unilever said that if Unilever only knew what it knows, it would double its profits. The meaning is clear: Many companies sit on rich information but fail to mine this information. This has led to an explosion of interest in *knowledge management*: organizing a company's information so that it is easily retrievable and learning can be extracted from it.

Many companies, especially those resulting from mergers or acquisitions, have ended up with incompatible data systems. Before they can get a whole view of their customer, competition, and distribution, they have to streamline and integrate their data into a single data system.

Marketing is becoming more based on information than on brute sales power. Thanks to the computer and the Internet, no salesperson can say to the boss that he or she didn't know the prospect's industry, company, problems, or potentials. Using *sales automation software*, a salesperson can record each prospect's and customer's needs, interests, opinions, and hot buttons. The salesperson can answer questions in the prospect's office by connecting with the company's mainframe or other resources on his or her laptop. The salesperson, after negotiating, can print out a customized contract for the prospect to sign. And afterward, the salesperson can look up what any customer bought and figure out further opportunities for cross-selling or up-selling.

Besides sales automation software, companies need *marketing automation software* to help their marketers gain efficiency and effectiveness.

One form is *real-time inventory management*, where a marketer can tell what the company and its competitors sold yesterday, including features and prices. This not only facilitates more synchronous production planning but also allows real-time tactical responses.

- Some people define Wal-Mart as an information system company more than a retailer. Wal-Mart knows the sales of each product in each store at the end of the day, making it easier to order the right replacement stock for the next day. The result: Wal-Mart carries lower inventory and therefore needs less working capital. Its ordering is driven by real demand, not by forecasted demand. It has synchronized its ordering with the demand flow.
- 7-Eleven in Japan is another retailer making data-driven decisions. 7-Eleven replenishes its stock three times a day in response to orders from individual store managers of what they expect to sell in the next few hours. 7-Eleven not only trains its store operators to capture customer and sales information but also teaches them how to use it.

Another form is *real-time selling*, where a company has programmed in rules suggesting other products and services that might be mentioned to a prospect or customer on the spot.

- Suppose a couple in their late forties comes into a bank for a home repair loan. Such customers are likely to have college-age children, and the bank might mention a college loan as well.

- A business traveler checks into a hotel that knows from her record that she is a frequent traveler. The hotel clerk might offer to arrange for her stays at sister hotels for known future dates.

Still another form is *marketing process automation*, where a company has codified its marketing processes that its product, brand, and segment managers need to know to operate more effectively.

- A brand manager needing to do a concept test turns on his computer and looks up the six steps in a concept test; he receives tips and best-of-class examples. A brand manager needing to choose an appropriate sales promotion turns to her computer to get world-class advice.

Yet another form is an assortment of software packages that facilitate handling such processes as new product development, advertising campaigns, marketing projects, and contract management. They are being developed by Emmperative, E.piphany, Unica, and several other marketing automation firms.

In all battles—military, business, and marital—victory goes to the party that has the better information. Arie De Geus, former strategist for Royal Dutch/Shell, observed: **"The ability to learn faster than our competitors may be our only sustainable competitive weapon."**

At the same time, managers often must make decisions before they have all the facts. If they wait too long, the opportunity may be gone.

Innovation

Firms face a dilemma. If they don't innovate, they will die. And if they do innovate—and their innovations are not successful—they may also die. Given that only 20 percent of consumer packaged goods introductions are successful and maybe 40 percent of new business-to-business products are successful, the odds are discouraging.

Yet innovation is a safer bet than standing still. The key is to manage innovation better than your competitors. Innovation and imagination must be made into a *capability*, as it is at 3M, Sony, Casio, Lexus, Braun, and Honda. These companies have been called "product juggernauts" in that they run product development as an ongoing and interactive process, with the manufacturer, sales force, and customer all working together to develop, refine, adapt, and improve products.[37]

The innovation process has to be managed carefully as a set of processes, including *idea development, idea screening, concept development and testing, business analysis, prototype development and testing, test marketing,* and *commercialization*. The company needs to build in or acquire the competencies needed in each step of the process. And it must appoint a well-seasoned leader of the innovation process.

Gary Hamel holds that innovation can be a *strategic capability*, just like in some companies quality is a discipline.[38] Innovation is not achieved by a two-day brainstorming session. Success requires developing three markets within the firm: an *idea market*, a *capital market*, and a *talent market*. The company must encourage and reward new ideas; it must set aside a pool of money to finance investments in promising new ideas; and it must attract the talent necessary to implement these ideas. And those who contributed the ideas, capital, and talent should be rewarded.

Innovation is not limited to new products or services. It includes thinking up new businesses and business processes. Nestlé sells coffee in the groceries but it was Starbucks that thought up a new way to retail coffee. Barnes & Noble thought up a new concept for a physical bookstore, and Amazon thought up a brilliant system for selling books online. All of the following were major business innovations: Club Med, CNN, Dell Computer, Disney, Domino's Pizza, Federal Express, IKEA, McDonald's, watchmaker Swatch, Wal-Mart.

A company needs to pursue both continuous improvement and discontinuous innovation. Continuous improvement is essential, but discontinuous innovation would be even better. A greater sustainable competitive advantage can come from discontinuous innovation, albeit at a much greater cost and risk. The risk comes from several facts: The technology is evolving, there are competing technologies, the market is ill-defined, there is no delivery infrastructure, and timing of completion is difficult. Furthermore, marketing research is of little value. Discontinuous innovation hurts the bottom line in the short term, and it may not help the bottom line in the long term. The conventional new product process works well for continuous improvements but does not work for discontinuous innovations.

Where should companies go to get new product ideas? A marketer's normal answer is to ask customers what they need. Done right, this can yield useful ideas, but probably incremental rather than breakthrough ideas. Consumers would not have answered that they wanted a PC, Palm, Walkman, wireless phone, or camcorder. Akio

Morita, Sony's late CEO, said: **"There was no need for market research. The public does not know what is possible. We do."**[39]

The truth is that ideas can come from anywhere, and not only from customers or the lab. Every firm is a potential hotbed of ideas, except the company fails to stimulate them or lacks a net to catch them. Why not appoint a high-level *idea manager* to whom salespeople, distributors, suppliers, and employees could send their ideas? The idea manager has a committee that finds the better ideas and rewards those whose ideas the company implements. The Dana Corporation, for example, expects every employee to place two ideas a month into the company's suggestion box on any improvements the employee senses, whether in selling, purchasing, energy use, travel, or other areas.

Companies that expect mild improvements can usually get them. The trick is to ask for a huge improvement. Instead of a 10 percent reduction in costs, ask for a 50 percent reduction in costs. Instead of a 10 percent improvement in productivity, ask for a tenfold improvement. The effect of this is to force everyone to reexamine the operation and design a better operation, instead of only squeezing out a little more from the present operation.

Every business should examine its *innovation index*. This describes the proportion of its sales derived from products less than three years old. No company will survive with a zero innovation index. A traditional business will have a hard time if its innovation index isn't at least 20 percent. High-fashion clothing businesses need at least a 100 percent innovation index to succeed. The message: *Innovate or evaporate.* (Also see Creativity, New Product Development.)

Intangible Assets

The modern balance sheet is a lie! It omits the company's most important assets. Probably 80 percent of a company's value lies in its intangible assets; but they are not on the books. The value of a company's plant, equipment, inventory, and working capital hardly reflects a true value of a company.

For example, where is Coca-Cola's *brand value* on the company's balance sheet? Coca-Cola's brand value is estimated at $70 billion. Where is the *value of its customer base*? It's the satisfied customers who repeatedly purchase from the firm who constitute a major asset. Where is *employee value*? Having better employees than the competition will spell the difference between having superior profits and average profits. Where is *partners value*? Loyal suppliers and distributors can make a company, and disloyal ones can break a company. Where is *knowledge and intellectual capital value*? Patents, copyrights, trademarks, and licenses can be one of the company's major assets.

No wonder there is often a huge gap between a company's market capitalization and its book value. The gap reflects the value of the intangibles. For example, AmericaOnline's book value in 1999 was only 3.3 percent of its market capitalization. Thus 97 percent of AOL's value was not on the balance sheet.

Companies would be wise if they start identifying and assessing all their marketing assets such as their brands, customer relationships, employee relationships, channel relationships, supplier relationships, and intellectual capital. The company should choose marketing activities that build the value of their market-based assets.

Should your company even consider owning physical assets? Owning physical property can be a liability. All a company needs is *access* to physical assets. To operate as a lean company may call for *decapitalizing*—outsourcing activities and shrinking working capital. The Sara Lee Corporation, for one, thinks that it is better to own brands (Champion, Coach, Hanes, Playtex, Hillshire Farm, and others) than factories.

International Marketing

A company that masters only its domestic market will eventually lose it. Strong foreign competitors will inevitably come in and challenge your company. It is now business without borders.

One of the best growth paths for a business is to go regional or global. But most companies hesitate to go abroad. They see obstacles and risks stemming from tariffs, language differences, cultural differences, devaluation and exchange control risk, and bribery.

But there are also gains. By going abroad, companies actually diversify their risks by not depending on only one country's market.

In fact, the market for their products and services may be mature at home and growing abroad. Furthermore, these companies will be stimulated to improve their products as they compete in new situations against new competitors.

But companies must adapt their products and marketing mix when they go abroad. Asea Brown Boveri (ABB) uses the slogan: **"We are a global firm local everywhere."** Royal Ahold, the giant Dutch food retailer, has the brand philosophy, **"Everything the customer sees we localize. Everything they don't see, we globalize."**

When naming its new products, a company must make sure its name will travel internationally. Chevrolet named its new car Nova, not realizing that in Latin America *no va* means "doesn't go."

Companies usually evolve globally through five stages: (1) passively exporting, (2) actively exporting using distributors, (3) opening sales offices abroad, (4) setting up factories abroad, and (5) establishing regional headquarters abroad.

In expanding abroad, companies tend to exercise loose administrative controls initially, preferring to put their faith in their entrepreneurial country managers. Later they start imposing some strategic controls aimed at standardizing global planning and decision processes.

Companies must choose foreign distributors carefully. They need to define distributor performance very clearly and be aware of host country laws regarding distributor treatment. The distributors need to be given adequate incentives to grow the market as fast as possible.

Companies succeed best when they recognize a large target market whose needs are not being met by the current sellers. By inventing new values for this target market that are difficult to replicate and by building a strong company culture to serve this market, the company has a good chance to succeed.

Companies entering developing countries should offer new benefits or introduce their products at a lower price, rather than come in with the same offerings made at home. They must be conscious of liability for the potential misuse of their products due to low literacy and the poor quality of intermediary channels, as well as counterfeiting possibilities.

Two issues arise when a company appoints regional managers. The first is whether to locate regional management at headquarters or in a capital city of the region. The second is whether regional managers should represent the interests of headquarters or of the region's country managers. The regional headquarters location will influence its orientation.

Although a company may grant high autonomy to its country managers, it can still achieve a fair measure of coordination through corporate information exchange systems, company guidelines and regulations, regional line managers, and headquarters product directors.

Country managers are not all equal. Usually the country managers in the larger markets have more autonomy and influence. The larger markets are often chosen as centers of excellence in the handling of research and development (R&D) and new product launches. They also have a large influence on the country managers in the smaller surrounding countries.

Multinational corporations face tough decisions on which products to emphasize in which countries. The allocation of products and advertising money to the different countries must be guided by consumer preferences and purchasing power, distribution strength, competitor positions, and economic future conditions in each country.

Highly efficient export-oriented companies are likely to gain market share in other countries. This will set up resistance by entrenched interests in the form of high tariffs and dumping charges. Ultimately these exporters may be wise to move production into countries that are resisting these imports.

A multinational that abandons troubled countries will have to eventually abandon all countries. The company should think more of shrinking its presence in a troubled country than abandoning it.

Global countries must learn to use countertrading. Many countries are poor but they will barter. You'd better learn to take some goods in exchange or forget selling to that country. Pepsi-Cola had to promise Russia that it would help sell Russian vodka abroad in exchange for selling Pepsi-Cola in Russia.

When companies fail abroad, the most common factors are:

- Failure to take enough time to observe, absorb, and learn the new market.
- Failure to get reliable statistical information about the new market.
- Failure to define the target user.
- Failure to adapt the product and/or marketing mix.
- Failure to offer adequate service.
- Failure to find good strategic partners.

Internet and E-Business

The Internet offers radically new possibilities for conducting business more efficiently. Just look at what you can do now that you couldn't have done (or done easily) before:

- You can display much more information about your company and products—and sell them—on a web site operating 24 hours a day, 7 days a week.
- You can purchase more effectively because you can use the Internet to identify more suppliers, put out requisitions online, buy on market exchanges, and hunt for bargains on online auction markets and used goods markets.
- You can place orders, transact, and make payments to suppliers and distributors faster and at a lower cost by setting up extranets with your partners.
- You can recruit more effectively using online job listing services and e-mail interviews.
- You can supply better information and training to employees and to your dealers through the Internet.
- You can set up an intranet to facilitate communication among your employees, as well as between them and headquarters and your mainframe computer. The intranet can feature

newsletters, personnel information, product information, e-learning modules, company calendars, and so on.

- You can promote your products over a much broader geographical area.
- You can more efficiently research markets, customers, prospects, and competitors by tapping into the wealth of information on the Internet and by carrying out focus groups and surveys on the Internet.
- You can send ads, coupons, samples, and information to requesting or targeted customers.
- You can customize offerings, services, and messages to individual customers.
- You can substantially improve your logistics and operations using the Internet.

The Internet provides a brilliant new platform for communicating, buying, and selling. Its benefits will only grow over time. Business leaders have lauded its potentials:

- Jack Welch of GE admonished his people to produce more than a web site: **"Embrace the Net. Bring me a plan how you are going to transform your business beyond adding an Internet site."**
- John Chambers, CEO of Cisco, aims to Web-ify Cisco's entire business: **"Every customer interaction provided by a Cisco employee that does not add value to the business ought to be replaced by a Web-based function."**
- Bill Gates, chairman of Microsoft, sees the Internet as indispensable to companies: **"The Internet is not just another sales channel. The future company will operate with a *digital nervous system*."**

By embracing the Internet early, companies have greatly reduced their costs compared to late-adopting competitors:

- Dell, by selling customized computers through low-cost telecommunications and Web channels, has a much lower cost of doing business than HP/Compaq, IBM, and Apple. Dell has grown at twice the rate of the rest of the industry and is now the leading personal computer seller in the United States.
- GE claims to have saved hundreds of millions of dollars of its purchasing budget by establishing its Trading Process Network and requisitioning products over the Internet.
- Oracle ran an ad claiming to have saved over a billion dollars by using its Internet-based systems in running its own business.

Although the main benefits of the Internet are many and varied, it was e-commerce and not the other applications that caught most of the public's attention. E-commerce meant the opportunity to convert the Internet into a selling channel. E-commerce dot.coms started by selling books, music, toys, electronics, stock buying, insurance, and airline tickets, and soon added furniture, large appliances, home banking, home food delivery, consulting, and almost everything else. The new dot.coms instilled fear in every store-based retailer. Would the availability of online products spell the kiss of death for stores?

Smart store-based retailers such as Barnes & Noble, Wal-Mart, and Levi's took no chances and set up separate online sales channels. Instead of staying only "brick and mortar," they moved to "brick and click."

But many dot.coms collapsed in the late 1990s, having made the mistake of collecting "eyeballs" instead of revenues. One dot.com start-up told the venture capital supplier: "Revenues are a distraction that I cannot afford." These dot.coms lacked not only an e-business strategy but even a business strategy.

No wonder so many dot.coms turned into dot.bombs. When the dot.com bubble burst, many store-based businesses gave a sigh of relief. Yet smart retailers and businesses did not ignore the potentials of the Internet and added an online presence.

Every company needs a web site today that reflects the company's quality. One warning: Don't let your web site be designed by a techie who wants to illustrate his or her technical prowess. Customers can't wait for all the downloading of pretty pictures. They want information, not show time. They want a fast download, a clear and uncluttered initial screen, easy passage to other screens, clear information, an easy ordering procedure, and no intrusive advertising.

Leadership

All managers should be leaders, but most are administrators. If you are spending most of your time on budgets, organization charts, costs, compliance, and detail, you are an administrator. To become a leader, you need to spend more time with people, scanning opportunities, developing a vision, and setting goals.

Your chief executive officer (CEO) should be the firm's architect; and your chief operating officer (COO) should be the firm's engineer who optimizes within the firm's architecture. To do their respective jobs well, both should have selling skills. They need to sell their ideas to their investors, peers, and staff. Leaders need to be teachers and teach others to be leaders.

Bad managers, in contrast, rely on command and control to get their ideas carried out.

A business leader's job is **"to make meaning"** (John Seely Brown, chief scientist of Xerox Corporation). The leader needs vision. Vision is **"the art of seeing things invisible"** (Jonathan Swift). Vision is the ability to conjure up a picture of great opportunities to inspire the employees and the company's stakeholders. The vision must burn in the leader's breast if it is to ignite a passion in others. At the same time, be warned that there is a big difference between vision and hallucination.

The leader must be able to gain respect for his vision and as a person. The followers must believe that the leader is serving them, that he or she is a *servant-leader*. Napoleon said that **"A leader is a dealer in hope."** Robert Townsend, former CEO of Avis Rent-A-Car, observed: **"True leadership must be for the benefit of the followers, not the enrichment of the leaders."** Leadership works best when there are committed followers.

Some think that great leaders need charisma, and point to people such as Franklin Roosevelt or Winston Churchill. They are forgetting Harry Truman. The leader does not need charisma to be effective. Charismatic leaders are often suspect. Some of the greatest business leaders went about their work in a quiet way touching the minds and hearts of their staff. They are friendly, approachable, and caring. They act as role models. Charles R. Walgreen III transformed Walgreen Co. into a company whose cumulative stock returns since 1975 have beaten the general stock market by over 15 times. Yet he never takes credit, pointing instead to his great team, and he pins his success on being "lucky." Katherine Graham of *The Washington Post* was another quiet leader who built a great newspaper into a greater one. The Chinese philosopher Lao-tzu said: **"A leader is best when people barely know that he exists."**[40]

The best leaders want to surround themselves with talented managers. They revel in finding managers who are smarter than they are. CEO Tom Siebel wants the executives in his organization to be significantly smarter than he is in their particular areas. The chief financial officer (CFO) should be better at managing finances than the

CEO, and the head of marketing should be better at marketing than the CEO. The CEO's main task is to build a team of experts who are aligned with each other and the primary goals of the company.

And good leaders don't want yes-men. Be ready to fire those who agree with you. Good leaders want the honest views of their colleagues. They encourage constructive debates and out-of-the-box thinking. They invite big-picture ideas. They tolerate honest mistakes. And when they make the final decision, they inspire their people to do their best.

And the best leaders don't spend too much time poring over numbers. They get out and meet the troops. And they devote a lot of time to major customers. Jack Welch of GE spent 100 days a year talking with major customers. So did Lou Gerstner of IBM.

At the same time, the job of a leader is daunting. It isn't all about playing golf with other business leaders. One CEO said, **"I am only comfortable when I am uncomfortable."** When Dick Ferris, former CEO of United Air Lines, was asked how he sleeps in tumultuous times, he said, **"Just like a baby—I wake up every two hours and cry."**

Yet the leader must be more of an optimist than a pessimist. He must see the cup as half full rather than half empty. He is mostly tested when the times are tough. It is a rough sea that can make a great captain. Clearly the leader lives with risks. Followers are lucky because all they have to do is carry out the orders.

Leaders can be corrupted by success. If they are not careful, egotism seeps in. As someone observed: **"Egotism is the quality that causes a person to think he's in the groove when he's actually in a rut."**

With regard to marketing, too many CEOs see marketing expenditures as just an expense and fail to see that a large part of it is an investment. There are two types of CEOs: those who know that they don't understand marketing and those who don't know that they don't understand marketing.

Loyalty

"Loyalty" is an old-fashioned word describing being deeply committed to one's country, family, or friends. It came into marketing with the term *brand loyalty*. But can people be loyal to a brand? Tony O'Reilly, former CEO of H. J. Heinz, proposed this test of brand loyalty: **"My acid test . . . is whether a housewife, intending to buy Heinz tomato ketchup in a store, finding it to be out of stock, will walk out of the store to buy it elsewhere."**

That some people will be exceptionally loyal to some brands is incontrovertible. The Harley Davidson motorcycle owner won't switch even if convinced that another brand performs better. Apple Macintosh users won't switch to Microsoft even if they could gain some advantages. BMW fans won't switch to Mercedes. We say that a company enjoys high brand loyalty when a sizable number of its customers won't switch.

Brand loyalty is roughly indicated by the company's customer retention rate. The average firm loses half its customers in less than five years. Firms with high brand loyalty may lose not more than 20 percent of their customers in five years. But a high retention rate may indicate other things than loyalty. Some customers stay on because of inertia or indifference or being held hostage to long-term contracts.

Building loyal customers requires a company to discriminate. We are not talking about racial, religious, or gender discrimination. We are talking about discriminating between profitable and unprofitable customers. No company can be expected to pay the same attention to an unprofitable customer as to a profitable customer. Smart companies define the types of customers they are seeking who would most benefit from the firm's offerings; these customers are the most likely to stay loyal. And loyal customers pay back the company in long-term cash flows and in generating a stream of referrals.

Some companies believe that they win customer loyalty by offering a **loyalty award program.** A loyalty program may be a good feature as part of a customer relationship management program, but many loyalty schemes do not create loyalty. They appeal to the customer's rational side of accumulating something free but do not necessarily create an emotional bond. How can frequent-flier miles win customer loyalty in the face of canceled flights, overcrowded planes, lost baggage, and indifferent cabin crews? Some programs are disloyalty programs, as when an airline says the points will be lost unless the customer flies within two months.

Companies should reward their loyal customers. Too often, however, companies give a better deal to new customers than to their old customers. Thus a telecom company may offer brand-new handsets and a reduced-price call plan to attract new customers while old customers are stuck with outdated handsets and pay more. Why not offer a trade-in plan for old equipment and a call plan that cost less each year that the customer stays with the company? State Farm Mutual Automobile Insurance does this, where each year the insured automobile owner gets a reduced rate if there are no claims.

While every company should aim to build loyal customers, loyalty is never so strong that customers can resist a competitor who shows up with a much stronger value proposition that gives customers everything they now have and more.

Management

Management is the task of making trade-offs and juggling contradictions. Harvard's Rosabeth Moss Kanter observed: **"The ultimate corporate balancing act: Cut back and grow. Trim down and build. Accomplish more, and do it in new areas, with fewer resources."**

Everyone in a company has a different agenda. The advertising manager sees the company's salvation as being in more advertising; the sales manager wants more salespeople; the sales promotion manager wants more money for incentives; and the R&D department wants more money for product improvement and new product development.

The problem is that if every department only does its own job well, the company will fail. Departments have individual agendas, not company agendas. The gift of *reengineering* thinking is to switch the focus away from departments toward managing core processes. Each core process—product development, customer attraction and retention, order fulfillment—requires teamwork from several departments. Increasingly major company initiatives are launched as interdisciplinary team projects, not department projects.

Management must never relax its vigilance. Business is a race without a finishing line. Andrew Grove, former CEO of Intel, postulated Grove's Law, **"Only the paranoid survive."** But the Japanese see management's task more positively and call it *kaizen*: **"Improving everything all the time by everyone."** They would rather improve their business every day than pray for an occasional breakthrough. The company that stops getting better gets worse.

At the same time, improving the efficiency of the current operations is not enough. Defining good management in this way has caused many businesses to fold. Management puts the company at risk by staying indoors and not wandering out. In viewing the business from inside out rather than from outside in, they miss changes in customers, competitors, and channels. They miss threats and opportunities. John Le Carré observed: **"A desk is a dangerous place from which to view the world."**

Most companies are managed by committees. Richard Harkness, a journalist, defined a committee as **"a group of the unwilling, picked from the unfit, to do the unnecessary."** Others say that committees are a fine device when you don't want to accomplish anything. Peter Drucker observed: **"Ninety percent of what we call 'management' is making it difficult to get things done."**

Every committee meeting should end in 45 minutes, or at least the attendees should take a vote to continue. Some say that the optimum size of a committee is zero. Former U.S. Senator Harry Chapman gave this advice about being on a committee:

1. Never arrive on time; this [punctuality] stamps you as a beginner.
2. Don't say anything until the meeting is half over; this stamps you as being wise.

3. Be as vague as possible; this avoids irritating the others.
4. When in doubt, suggest that a subcommittee be appointed.
5. Be the first to move for adjournment; this will make you popular; it's what everyone is waiting for.

Marketing Assets and Resources

Companies think that they have a complete list of their assets on their balance sheets: physical assets, accounts receivable, working capital, and the like. But their real assets are off balance sheet items such as the value of their *brands, employees, distribution partners, suppliers,* and *intellectual knowledge* including patents, trademarks, and copyrights.

You need to go further and list your *core competencies* and *core processes* as assets. Any special skills and proprietary processes are assets. Strategy is essentially the way a company chooses to link its competencies, core processes, and other assets to win marketplace battles.

At the same time, don't limit your search for opportunities by starting with your assets and resources. First look outside the firm for your opportunities, and then see if you have or can attract the needed resources and competencies. I have always been impressed with 3M's willingness to go after a promising opportunity even if it lacked the requisite resources. You can always buy or outsource them.

Marketing Department Interfaces

Each company department carries images or stereotypes of the other departments. Most often they are not flattering. Furthermore, the departments compete for the available resources, each making the case that it can spend the money better. All this interferes with harmonious working relations between departments.

Some members of other departments will stereotype the marketing department as consisting of fast-talking salespeople who cajole a large budget from management without providing any evidence of its impact, as con men who snare customers with a dishonest pitch, or as hucksters pressing R&D for new bells and whistles rather than for real product improvements.

One engineer complained that the salespeople are "always protecting the customer and not thinking of the company's interest!" He also blasted customers for "asking for too much."

Marketers, in turn, are critical of other departments:

- Marketers have difficulties with engineers. Engineers tend to be exact in their thinking, seeing black and white and missing shades of gray. They tend to describe the product in highly technical terms rather than in language that most customers would understand.

   In high-tech companies, the engineers are king. The engineers look askance at any engineers who went into sales, concluding that they must be poorly trained. If they went into customer service, they were really losers.

- Marketers see their immediate enemy as the finance people who demand that marketers justify each expense item, and who hold back as much funds from marketing as possible. Finance people think mainly of current-period performance and fail to understand that a large part of marketing expenditures are investments, not expenses, that build long-term brand strength. When the company hits a slump, finance people's first step is to cut the marketing budget, implying that the funds aren't necessary. The antidote is to work closely with finance to develop financial models of how marketing investments impact revenues, costs, and profits.

- Marketing people complain about the purchasing people if they buy cheaper inputs that result in the product not having the quality promised in the value proposition. True, the purchasing people must keep input costs low, but controls must be established to ensure sufficient quality.

   I advise marketers to work more closely with the purchasing people not only to ensure good quality but to learn from them about selling. Purchasing people are experts at what makes good salesmanship. Why? Because purchasing people are approached all day long by salespeople and can tell stories about the difference between effective and poor selling styles.

It would be good training for marketers to work in purchasing for a while to learn how to deal with salespeople.

General Electric once developed a game to be played between its own purchasing and sales personnel to see who would be more effective. The purchasing people won hands down. GE's management then said: "If our salespeople cannot sell effectively to our own purchasing people, how can they sell effectively to our customers' purchasing people?"

- Marketers have only a few issues with the manufacturing people. They hope that the manufacturing people produce the products at the specified quality level so that the customers aren't disappointed. They also ask manufacturing to make special short runs or add custom features, but here they encounter some resistance. Manufacturing costs rise when production changes must be frequently made.

- Marketers find it hard to communicate with information technology (IT) people. The marketers talk sales, market share, and margin, while the IT people talk COBOL, Java, Linus, and tetrabytes. The big mistake is when marketing asks IT to develop a database marketing system, only to regret commissioning it in the first place once it is finished. Yet marketing needs database software and supply chain software if customers are to be served well. Clearly, marketing departments need to add a technical marketer who understands information technology and can mediate between the two groups.

- Marketers get upset with the credit department when credit refuses to approve a transaction on the grounds that the prospect might default. The salesperson worked hard to get the sale only to find that he or she can't put it through and get recognition for the sale.

- Marketers are annoyed with the accountants who are slow in answering customer questions about their invoices. Marketers would also like the accountants to give them better measures of the profitability of different geographical areas, market segments, channels, and individual customers. This information would help marketers allocate their efforts closer to the areas of greater profit.

- Even within the larger marketing group, there are frictions between marketing, the sales force, and customer service. Marketing began as a function to help the sales force sell better. Marketing helped by getting leads through advertising, brochures, and other communications. Later, marketing gathered information to estimate market potential, assign sales quotas, and develop sales forecasts. Salespeople often have complained about marketing setting sales quotas or company prices too high, saying that more money should go to the sales force (and less to advertising) to raise their compensation or to hire more salespeople. When marketing and sales get into conflict, sales often wins because salespeople are responsible for short-term results.

   As for customer service, this has typically been treated as less important than getting the sale. When customers complained to customer service, salespeople could resent the watchdog role customer service plays, although good customer service is in their best interest in the long run.

The fact is that these departments are in active competition for a limited budget, each making the case that they can spend the money better. Each department also wants to feel important and respected by the other groups.

The challenge is how to break down departmental walls and harmonize the efforts of different departments to work as a team. Here are two approaches:

1. Companies would hold meetings of two departments at a time to express their views of each other's strengths and weaknesses and offer their suggestions for how to improve their relationship.
2. Companies are increasingly managing processes rather than functions and putting together cross-disciplinary teams to manage these processes. The various members begin to appreciate each other's point of view, and hopefully this produces better understanding.

arketing Ethics

Companies often must choose between taking the high road and making the decent decision versus taking the low road and breaching their customers' trust. Tylenol took the high road when someone tampered with its pills. It immediately recalled and destroyed its stock. Intel took the middle road because it hesitated to replace a chip that had a minor defect. Ford on occasions has taken the low road by denying faults with some of its cars.

Business practices are often under attack because business situations routinely pose tough ethical dilemmas. One can go back to Howard Bowen's classic questions about the responsibilities of a businessperson:

Should he conduct selling in ways that intrude on the privacy of people, for example, by door-to-door selling . . . ? Should he use methods involving ballyhoo, chances, prizes, hawking, and other tactics which are at least of doubtful good taste? Should he employ "high pressure" tactics in persuading people to buy? Should he try to hasten the obsolescence of goods by bringing out an endless succession of new models and new styles? Should he appeal to and attempt to strengthen the motives of materialism, invidious consumption, and "keeping up with the Joneses"?[41]

The most admired companies abide by a code of serving people's interests, not only their own. The Reputation Institute and Harris Interactive collect ratings by the public on the companies they admire the most. The top 15 in 2001 (in order) are Johnson & Johnson, Microsoft, Coca-Cola, Intel, 3M, Sony, Hewlett-Packard, FedEx, Maytag, IBM, Disney, General Electric, Dell, Procter & Gamble, and United Parcel Service (UPS). These companies are notable for their products, service levels, and corporate philanthropy. Their reputations and trustworthiness add to their pocketbooks.

Marketing Mix

Marketing mix describes the set of tools that management can use to influence sales. The traditional formulation is called the 4Ps—product, price, place, and promotion.

From the very beginning questions were raised about the 4P formulation of the marketing mix.

- Perfume companies wanted packaging to be added as a fifth P. 4P guardians said that packaging is already in the scheme, under product.
- Sales managers asked whether the sales force was left out because it began with an S. No, said the guardians, sales force is a promotion tool, along with advertising, sales promotion, public relations, and direct marketing.
- Service managers asked where services were in the marketing mix, or whether they, too, were excluded because the first letter was S. Here the guardians said services are part of the product. As services grew more important, service marketers suggested adding three Ps to the original 4Ps, namely *personnel*, *procedures*, and *physical evidence*. Thus a restaurant's performance will depend on its staff, the process by which it

serves food (buffet, fast food, tablecloths, etc.), and its physical looks and features as a restaurant.

- Others suggested adding *personalization* to the marketing mix. The marketer has to decide how personalized to make the product, the price, the place, and the promotion.
- In my own case, I suggested adding politics and public relations to the 4Ps, because these can also influence a company's ability to sell.
- At one time, I had also proposed escaping from the prison of the letter P by redefining the essential function of each P:

Product   = Configuration
Price   = Valuation
Place   = Facilitation
Promotion = Symbolization

A more basic criticism has been that the 4Ps represent the seller's mind-set, not the buyer's mind-set. Robert Lauterborn suggested that sellers should first work with 4Cs before setting the 4Ps.[42] The 4Cs are customer value (not product), customer costs (not price alone), convenience (not place), and communication (not promotion). Once the marketer thinks through the 4Cs for the target customer, it becomes much easier to set the 4Ps.

The Ps can substitute for each other in driving sales. A car dealer sold cars with 10 salespeople and normal markups. His sales were poor. Then he cut his staff to five salespeople and lowered his car prices significantly. He did a land-office business. Similarly, Jeff Bezos, CEO of Amazon, reduced his advertising expenditures and lowered his book prices, and Amazon's sales shot up significantly.

Setting the 4Ps is difficult because of their interactions. Take product and place:

- Suppose product is 0 and place is 1. How much is 0×1? Answer = 0.

- Suppose product is 1 and place is 0. How much is 1×0? Answer = 0.
- Suppose product is 1 and place is 1. How much is 1×1? Answer = 3.

One selects marketing tools that are appropriate to the stage of the *product's life cycle*. For example, advertising and publicity will produce the biggest payoff in the introduction stage of a product; their job is to build consumer awareness and interest. Sales promotions and personal selling grow more important during a product's maturity stage. Personal selling can strengthen customers' comprehension of your product's advantages and their conviction that the offering is worthwhile. Sales promotions are most effective for trig-

The marketing vice president of a major European airline wanted to increase the airline's traffic share. His strategy was to build up customer satisfaction through providing better food, cleaner cabins, better trained cabin crews, and lower fares. Yet he had no authority in these matters. The catering department chose food that kept down food costs; the maintenance department used cleaning services that kept down cleaning costs; the human resources department hired flight crew people without regard to whether they were naturally friendly; the finance department set the fares. Because these departments generally took a cost or production point of view, the vice president of marketing was stymied in creating an integrated marketing mix.

gering purchases today. In the decline stage, the company should keep pushing sales promotions but reduce advertising, publicity, and personal selling.

The choice of tools is also influenced by company size. Market leaders can afford more advertising and use sales promotion more sparingly. Smaller competitors, in contrast, use sales promotion more aggressively.

Consumer marketers tend to emphasize advertising over personal selling, and business marketers do the reverse. But both tools are required in both types of markets. Consumer marketers who emphasize *push strategies* need their sales force to convince retailers or dealers to carry, promote, and sell the company's product to end users. By contrast, consumer marketers who emphasize *pull strategies* rely heavily on advertising and consumer promotions to draw customers into stores.

For marketing to work, you must manage the marketing mix in an integrated fashion. Yet in many companies, responsibility for different elements of the marketing mix are in the hands of different individuals or departments.

Marketing Plans

Your company needs a vision, the vision demands a strategy, the strategy requires a plan, and the plan requires action. A Japanese proverb says: **"Vision without action is a daydream. Action without vision is a nightmare."**

You need to prepare a detailed marketing plan. But it makes more sense to call it a *battle plan*. Your plan should give you confidence that you will win the war before you engage in the first battle. If you aren't introducing something better, newer, faster, or cheaper, you shouldn't enter the market.

A marketing plan consists of six steps: situational analysis, objectives, strategy, tactics, budget, and controls.

1. *Situational analysis.* Here the company examines the *macro forces* (economic, political-legal, social-cultural, technological) and the *actors* (company, competitors, distributors, and suppliers) in its environment. The company carries out a SWOT analysis (strengths, weaknesses, opportunities, and threats). But it should really be called a TOWS analysis (threats, opportunities, weaknesses, and strengths) because the ordering should be from the outside in rather than the

inside out. SWOT may place an undue emphasis on internal factors and limit the identification of threats and opportunities to only those that fit the company's strengths.

2. *Objectives.* Based on identifying its best opportunities from its situational analysis, the company ranks them and sets goals and a timetable for achieving them. The company also sets objectives with respect to stakeholders, company reputation, technology, and other matters of concern.

3. *Strategy.* Any goal can be pursued in a variety of ways. It is the job of strategy to choose the most effective course of action for attaining objectives.

4. *Tactics.* The strategy must be spelled out in great detail regarding the 4Ps and the actions that will be taken in calendar time by specific individuals who are to carry out the plan.

5. *Budget.* The company's planned actions and activities involve costs that add up to the budget that it needs to achieve the its objectives.

6. *Controls.* The company must set review periods and measures that will reveal whether it is making progress toward the goal. When performance lags, the company must revise its objectives, strategies, or actions to correct the situation.

To facilitate the planning process, your company should work out a standard plan format to be used by all the divisions and product groups. This will make it possible for the plans to be reviewed, compared, and evaluated by the planning or strategy office. One large multinational corporation has a planning office that scores the various plans before they are approved. The office applies such criteria as:

- Is the situational analysis fairly complete?
- Are the goals reasonable and reachable in the light of the situational analysis?
- Does the strategy seem adequate to deliver the stated goals?

- Are the tactics well aligned with the stated strategy?
- Is the expected return on investment sufficient and credible?

Deficient plans are returned to division or product groups for revision along suggested lines. The use of a standard software planning program enables the planners to quickly revise their plans in response to criticism or unforeseen circumstances. In an advanced case, a company builds a model to estimate how hypothetical revisions in its advertising budget, sales force size, or prices will affect sales and profits. The Hudson River Group, for example, has developed *marketing strategy simulators* for different companies to help guide the allocation of marketing resources to their best uses.

The benefit of planning may lie less in the plan than in the process of planning. Dwight Eisenhower observed: **"In preparing for battle I have always found that plans are useless but planning is indispensable."**

No battle plan survives the first battle. It will need constant revision as the battle proceeds. You may have to redesign your airplane while you are in the air.

Make sure that you are not spending more time preparing plans than achieving results. Professor James Brian Quinn noted: **"A good deal of corporate planning . . . is like a ritual rain dance. It has no effect on the weather that follows."** The battle plan is nothing unless it progresses into work. Plan your work and work your plan. Marketing plans will not produce a dollar of profit if you don't implement them. But don't confuse motion with action.

Winning companies are those that do more of the right things (effectiveness) and do them better (efficiency).

Marketing Research

Marketing research in the early days was aimed more at finding techniques to increase sales than to understand customers. Researchers applauded the development of store audits, warehouse withdrawals, and consumer panels to provide needed information on product movement.

Over time, marketers increasingly recognized the importance of understanding buyers. Focus groups, questionnaires, and surveys came into vogue. Today the marketer's mantra is about the importance of understanding buyers at either the segment or the individual level. According to an old Spanish saying, **"To be a bullfighter, you must first learn to be a bull."**

Today's marketers use a whole bevy of marketing research techniques to understand customers and markets and their own marketing effectiveness. Here are some of the major research techniques in use:

- *In-store observation*. Paco Underhill, author of *Why We Buy*, runs Environsell to study in-store customer behavior.[43] His researchers use clipboards, track sheets, and video equipment to record the movements of shoppers. They are "retail anthropologists" studying over 70,000 shoppers a year in their "natural habitat." The findings include:

- Shoppers almost invariably walk to the right.
- Women are more likely to avoid narrow aisles than men.
- Men move faster than women through store aisles.
- Shoppers slow down when they see reflective surfaces and speed up when they see blanks.
- Shoppers don't notice elaborate signs in the first 30 feet of the entrance.

- *In-home observation*. Companies send researchers into homes to study household behavior toward products. Whirlpool arranged for an anthropologist to visit several homes to study how household members use large appliances. Ogilvy & Mather sent researchers with handheld videocameras into homes to prepare a 30-minute "highlight reel" of in-home behavior toward different products.

- *Other observation*. Observation can take place anywhere. Japanese carmakers stood in supermarket parking lots watching American women strain to lower their groceries into their car trunks and came up with a better trunk design. McDonald's executives once a year "work the counters" to experience customers firsthand. Marketers can learn a great deal by "stapling themselves to a customer."

- *Focus group research*. Companies frequently recruit one or more focus groups to talk about a product or service under the direction of a skilled moderator. The focus group may number 6 to 10 members who spend a few hours responding to the moderator's questions and to each other's comments. The session is usually videotaped and discussed later by a management team. While focus groups are an important preliminary step in exploring a subject, the results lack projectability to the larger population and should be treated cautiously.

- *Questionnaires and surveys.* Companies gather more representative information by interviewing a larger sample of the target population. The sample is drawn using statistical techniques, and the persons are reached either in person or by phone, fax, mail, or e-mail. The questionnaires typically ask questions that are codable and countable so as to yield a quantitative picture of customer opinions, attitudes, and behavior. By including personal questions, the surveyor can correlate the answers with different demographic and psychographic characteristics of the respondents. In using the findings, the company should be aware of possible biases resulting from a low response rate, poorly worded questions, or faults in the interviewing process and setting.

- *In-depth interviewing techniques.* Questionnaires are considered by some to be naive "nose counting" and their preference is to go deeper into the minds and motivations of consumers (often called "head shrinking"). Years ago, Ernest Dichter, who was trained as a Freudian, set a pattern of "motivational research" where he would enter into deep discussions with respondents to discern unconscious or repressed motivations. His findings, though interesting, were sometimes bizarre. For example, he concluded that consumers resist prunes because prunes are wrinkled and remind people of old age; therefore advertisers should feature "happy young prunes." And women don't trust cake mixes unless adding an egg is required so that homemakers can feel that they are giving "birth" to a "live cake." Dichter's findings lacked "scientific evidence" and "projectibility" but were always of interest to marketers and advertisers.[44]

A more recent technique, the Zaltman Metaphor Elicitation Technique (ZMET), developed by Professor Gerald Zaltman, seeks to bypass the verbal left brain and dip into the right brain and unconscious. ZMET asks small groups of consumers to collect pictures, create collages, and discuss these in an interview. ZMET claims to achieve insight into product themes and concerns that do not emerge through verbal research.[45]

- *Marketing experiments.* The most scientific way to research customers is to present different offerings to matched customer groups and analyze differences in their responses. Using split cable television or mail, companies are able to feature different ad headlines, prices, or promotions to see which one(s) draw better. To the extent that extraneous variables are controlled, the company can attribute response differences to offering differences.

- *Mystery shopper research.* Companies hire mystery shoppers to check on how well sales clerks handle difficult questions from customers, how well telephone operators answer phone calls, how easy it is to locate merchandise in a store, and many other uses. Mystery shopping is used to evaluate a company or competitor's marketing effectiveness rather than to understand customers' needs or wants.

- *Data mining.* Companies with large customer databases can use statisticians to detect in the mass of data new segments or new trends that the company can exploit.

Remember, marketing research is the first step and the foundation for effective marketing decision making. Herbert Baum, CEO of Hasbro Inc., said: **"Market research is crucial to a corporation's marketing process. I don't think anybody ought to be making marketing decisions without some form of research, because you can waste a lot of time and money."**

Marketing Roles and Skills

The marketing department's role in too many companies has been limited to carrying out marketing communications. R&D invents the product, and marketing writes the press releases and does the advertising. Too many CEOs think marketing comes into play only after the product has been made and must be sold. Marketing is run like a one-night stand instead of a long affair.

In this case, it would be better to operate two marketing groups, one doing strategy and the other doing tactics. Unless marketing is set up to have an effect on corporate strategy, its promise won't be fulfilled. In fact, I would argue that marketing's main role in the company is to be the driver of corporate strategy and the enforcer of the company's promises to its customers.

For this to happen, companies must move from *tactical* to *holistic marketing*.

- The company needs to enlarge its view of its customers' needs and lifestyles. The company should stop seeing the customer only as a consumer of its current products and start visualizing broader ways to serve its customers.

119

- The company needs to assess how all of its departments impact on customer satisfaction. Customers are adversely affected when their products arrive late or are damaged, when invoices are inaccurate, when customer service is poor, or when other foul-ups occur.
- The company needs to take a larger view of the company's industry, its players and its evolution. Today many industries are converging (e.g., telecommunications, entertainment, cable, the media, and software), presenting new opportunities and new threats to each industry player.
- The company needs to assess the impact of its actions on all the company's stakeholders—customers, employees, distributors, dealers, and suppliers—not only its shareholders. Any alienated stakeholder group can cause disruption to the company's plans and progress.

So what should be the major roles of marketers with respect to customers? At least the following:

- Detecting and evaluating new opportunities.
- Mapping customer perceptions, preferences, and requirements.
- Communicating customer wants and expectations to product designers.
- Making sure that customer orders are filled correctly and delivered on time.
- Checking that customers have received proper instructions, training, and technical assistance in the use of the product.
- Staying in touch with customers after the sale to ensure that they are satisfied.
- Gathering customer ideas for product and service improvements and conveying them to the appropriate departments.

What marketing skills do marketers need in order to carry out their role? J. S. Armstrong, a professor at the Wharton School, University of Pennsylvania, lists the following skills: *forecasting, planning, analyzing, creating, deciding, motivating, communicating*, and *implementing*. These skills make up what we call *marketing ability*, and it is marketing ability that companies look for in their search for a marketing vice president.

Markets

Markets can be defined in different ways. Originally a market was a physical place where buyers and sellers gathered. Economists describe a market as a collection of buyers and sellers who transact (in person, over the phone, by mail, whatever) over a particular product or product class. Thus economists talk about the car market or the housing market. But marketers view the sellers as the "industry" and the buyers as the "market." Thus marketers will talk about markets of "35 to 50-year-old low-income homemakers" or "auto company purchasing agents who buy paint for their companies."

Clearly markets can be defined broadly or narrowly. The "mass market" is the broadest definition and describes the billions of people who buy and consume basic products (e.g., soap, soft drinks). Much of U.S. economic growth has resulted from American companies mastering mass production, mass distribution, and mass marketing.

At the other extreme we can talk about a "market of one" to describe a specific individual or company that a marketer may be concerned with. IBM would be called a market of one for consultants who spend all of their time selling their services only to IBM.

The key point is that the marketer needs to define the *target market* as carefully as possible. The "mass market" is too vague. It is hard to make a product that everyone will want. It is easier to make a product that some will love. This has led businesses to pursue niches and mini-markets. But the downside is that as markets become sliced into finer segments, the resulting low volume in each will permit only one or a few companies to survive in that market.

Markets are often contrasted to hierarchies as a way of getting things done. Markets involve people entering into voluntary agreements that will leave both parties better off. Hierarchies, on the other hand, consist of people of high rank ordering those of lower rank to perform actions. Relying on markets rather than hierarchies is thought by many to be the best way to build a sustainable self-regulating economy. Command-and-control economies have not worked.

Marketing is a democratizing force. There are only four ways to obtain something that you want: *steal, borrow, beg,* or *exchange.* Using exchange (giving something to get something) is the most moral and efficient way and is the heart of marketing.

One thing is sure: Markets change faster than marketing. Buyers change in their numbers, wants, and purchasing power in response to changes in the economy, technology, and culture. Companies often don't notice these changes and maintain marketing practices that have lost their edge. The marketing practices of many companies today are obsolete.

Media

A company must use media. If your company doesn't use media, for all practical purposes your company doesn't exist.

The major media include television, radio, newspapers, magazines, catalogs, direct mail, telephone, and online. Each medium has its advantages and disadvantages in terms of cost, reach, frequency, and impact. An advertising agency devotes a major department to the work of finding the best media for attaining a given level of reach, frequency, and impact for a given budget. (See Advertising.)

At one time a company was able to reach 90 percent of the U.S. audience by advertising only on ABC, NBC, and CBS. Today it is lucky if these three media channels can reach 50 percent of the audience. Companies have to parcel out their budgets over dozens of media channels and vehicles. That's why targeting is critical. The mass market cannot be reached inexpensively anymore.

Media people are always searching for new media vehicles that are more cost-effective or attention-getting. They are now putting your ads on blimps and racing cars, and in elevators, bathrooms, and next to gas pumps. Yet as ads proliferate, they are in danger of being less noticed.

Your media efficiency can be greatly enhanced by moving toward database marketing. Not only can you send offers to selected members in your customer database, but you can buy additional names from *list brokers*. These brokers offer thousands of lists, such as "women executives earning over $100,000," "business professors teaching marketing," and "motorcycle owners." You can test a sample of names from a promising list. If the response rate is high, buy more names on the list; if low, don't use that list. You can reach the chosen prospects by phone, mail, fax, or e-mail. The good news is that you can measure the return on your advertising investment. **The future of media lies not in more broadcasting, but in more narrowcasting.**

Mission

Companies are set up to achieve a mission. They word their mission in various ways:

- Dell's mission: **"To be the most successful computer company in the world at delivering the best customer experience in the markets we serve."**
- Mars Company's mission: **"The consumer is our boss, quality is our work, and value is our goal."**
- McDonald's mission: **"Our vision is to be the world's best 'quick service restaurant.' This means opening and run-**

ning great restaurants and providing exceptional quality, service, cleanliness and value (QSCV)."

Virgin Atlantic Airways' success is partly due to redefining its business as entertainment, rather than just transportation. Virgin helps its passengers avoid a boring flight by supplying personal videos, massages, ice cream, and other treats only later imitated by its major competitors.

Johnson & Johnson prefers to prioritize its goals: **Its first responsibility is to its customers, its second to its employees, its third to its community, and its fourth to its stockholders.** This ordering of priorities is the best way to ensure profits for the stockholders, as J&J has proved over the years.

Most mission statements contain the right phrases: "People are our most important asset." "We will be the best at what we do." "We aim to exceed expectations." "We aim to make above average returns for our shareholders." The lazy way to prepare the mission statement is to assemble these in any order.

Print your mission statement on the back of your business card to remind your people, your prospects, and your customers of what your company stands for.

New Product Development

William H. Davidow, former Vice President of Strategy at Intel, got it right: **"While great devices are invented in the laboratory, great products are invented in the Marketing Department."** A product must be more than a physical device: It must be a concept that solves someone's problems.

And the product must eventually leave the laboratory and enter the market. Therefore it needs "landing gear as well as wings."

A high percentage of a new product's probable success can be determined before development is begun by answering three questions: "Do people need the product? Is it different and better than the competitors' offerings? Would people be willing to pay the price?" If the answer to any question is no, don't start the development project. *Never enter a battle before you are sure that you can win the war.*

The chances that the new product will be a hit are greatly enhanced if it represents a new product that defines a new category, such as the Palm, the Razor scooter, or Viagra. These products come with a ready-made story that will get the media talking about it. These products should be launched with PR, not with expensive "big bang" advertising. Media talk has much more credibility than any paid-for ads.

Ingvard Kamprad, who founded IKEA, added another consideration: **"A new idea without an affordable price tag is never acceptable."** Space Adventures offers to send you into space as an astronaut. Great! What's the price? $20 million! So far, there have been only two buyers.

Even with the right price tag, the money might really be made by a follow-on product. Earl Wilson, the columnist, observed: **"Benjamin Franklin may have discovered electricity, but it was the man who invented the meter who made the money."** By analogy, it was Xerox in its Palo Alto Research Center (PARC) that invented Ethernet, the graphical user interface, and the laser printer and yet it was Netscape, Apple, and Hewlett-Packard that made the money.

If it takes more than three years to develop a new product, it may not be the right product. Unfortunately, most companies cannot resist throwing good money after bad.

Who should ultimately design the product? R&D? Engineering? Manufacturing? Marketing? No! All of them, with the customer's help.

Customers expect improved products as well as new ones. Yet companies ask: "Why fix a product before it is broken?" My answer is that every competitor is scouting your product to find its weaknesses. It's important to fix your product before they do. Every company should obsolete its products before competitors do. Companies tend to pay too much attention to the cost of doing something when they should pay more attention to the cost of not doing it.

Who should be held accountable for a new product's results? Probably the research and development department and the marketing department—certainly not the sales department.

pportunity

The world abounds in opportunities, large and small. We are still waiting for a cure for cancer, tasty nonfattening foods, weight-loss schemes that work, and flying cars to avoid congested roads. While waiting, we can focus on trying to make our present products and services better in a hundred ways.

Look for problems. People complain about it being hard to sleep through the night, get rid of clutter in their homes, find an affordable vacation, trace their family origins, get rid of garden weeds, and so on. Each problem can spark several solutions. As the late John Gardner, founder of Common Cause, observed: **"Every problem is a brilliantly disguised opportunity."**

Look for trends. Surely you can get some ideas from Faith Popcorn's list of 16 trends, including *cocooning*, *down-aging*, and *cashing out*. Cocooning refers to people spending more time in their homes because the outside world is getting rough; therefore, think of ways to make the home more pleasant through furnishings, electronics, and entertainment. Down-aging captures the fact that older people want to feel young; hence the explosion of wrinkle creams, plastic surgery, and Jaguar sales. And cashing out means that people want to lead a less hectic existence and seek simpler lifestyles and smaller towns.

Don't just talk about opportunities. Success happens when preparation meets opportunity. A company has to either make history or become history. Someone compared market demand to a swiftly running stream: If you don't throw your line in fast enough, you won't catch the fish. Mark Twain learned this from bitter experience: **"I was seldom able to see an opportunity until it had ceased to be one."**

One of the greatest opportunities today is to invent businesses that can charge significantly lower prices than competitors and still be profitable. This has been the secret of Wal-Mart, Southwest Airlines, IKEA, and Dollar General. They reinvented their respective industries so as to be able to offer significantly lower prices than their competitors. Given the vast and growing number of low-income families, these retailers attracted millions of loyal customers.

Rosabeth Moss Kanter, in her *When Giants Learn to Dance*, observed: **"The years ahead will be best for those who learn to balance dreams and discipline. The future will belong to those who embrace the potential of wider opportunities but recognize the realities of more constrained resources, and find new solutions that permit doing more with less."**[46]

Said Ralph Waldo Emerson: **"This time, like all times, is a great time if we but know what to do with it."**

Organization

Who should headquarters work for? The field people, of course. The job of headquarters is to help the field people be the very best they can be. Robert Potter, past president of Monsanto Chemical Company, said: **"The division managers pay for the headquarters services from their own budgets. If they think they're paying too much for support staff, we simply eliminate the [headquarters] job."**

The sales department isn't the whole company, but the whole company had better be the sales department. Not everyone in a company is a marketing manager, but everyone should be in marketing management. This point is mentioned by Hiroyuki Takeuchi about Japanese companies: **"Fifty percent of Japanese companies do not have a marketing department, and ninety percent have no special section for marketing research. The reason is that everyone is considered to be a marketing specialist."**

Companies are organized vertically, but processes are horizontal. This is the mismatch that *reengineering* hopes to correct by appointing cross-disciplinary teams to manage key processes. (See Marketing Department Interfaces.)

Multidivisional companies tend to be product-oriented rather than industry- or customer-oriented. Yet the divisions may make products that go to the same industry or customer. Siemens recently developed a focus on four industries: hospitals, airports, stadiums, and university campuses. Siemens has assigned for each industry a single senior-level manager to have authority and accountability to orchestrate interdivisional cooperation regarding each industry.

Outsourcing

Your company can be great at only a few things. For the other things, hire those who can do these things better. Outsourcing originally applied only to the company's noncore activities, such as office cleaning and landscaping. But today's mantra is that a company should outsource everything that other parties can do better or more cheaply. Outsourcers are able to offer lower costs and better results because of their scale and specialization. Thus Nike decided not to manufacture its own shoes; Nike hires Asian firms that can produce shoes more cheaply and better.

Companies need to know which marketing activities to keep in-house versus outsourcing them. They usually outsource advertising services and marketing research. Some are now outsourcing direct mail services and telemarketing. A few are outsourcing new product development and a sales force. I know of companies that have outsourced their entire marketing department.

A company hired me to help management decide what to outsource. After examining all of their activities, I delivered a report to the board. "Gentlemen, you should outsource everything. You are not good at anything." They were stunned. "Are you saying that we should go out of business?" "No," I said. "I am telling you how to make more money. Your costs will go way down. The only competence you need is to manage outsourcers." Essentially I was proposing that they become a *virtual organization*.

Yet a company may go too far in outsourcing. What makes a great company is that it has created a set of core competencies that link ingeniously and would be difficult to imitate in total. This is what companies such as IKEA, Wal-Mart, and Southwestern Airlines have done. They have outsourced some activities, but what makes these companies great is they have reserved for themselves an interrelated set of competencies and capabilities that defy ready imitation.

Performance Measurement

Marketers have traditionally focused on a company's *sales, market share*, and *margin* to set its objectives and judge its performance. But gains in market share, while desirable, need further examination. Did you gain the right or wrong kinds of customers? Are they the staying or the switching kind? Are you "buying" share or "earning" it? Are you gaining a greater share of a shrinking market? Consider the following:

- Years ago General Electric fired a division manager because he grew his share of the vacuum tube market when he should have pursued the transistor market.
- Jack Welch said when he retired from GE that he had been wrong about needing to be number one or two in every business because "it leads management teams to define their markets narrowly . . . and has caused GE to miss opportunities and growth."

Focusing on margins can also be misleading. U.S. automakers resisted making good small cars because the margins were small. The Japanese went after this market knowing that they could capture the hearts of new young customers who would eventually buy larger Japanese cars.

133

Your company needs a whole set of additional measures to set its goals and gauge its performance (see box).

Your company must set more specific performance goals and measures for different marketing areas. For service support, you can use "on-time, first-time fix" to know the percentage of times the service person arrived on time and fixed the product perfectly. For order

---

Goals and Performance Measures

- Percentage of new customers to average number of customers.
- Percentage of lost customers to average number of customers.
- Percentage of win-back customers to average number of customers.
- Percentage of customers falling into very dissatisfied, dissatisfied, neutral, satisfied, and very satisfied categories.
- Percentage of customers who say they would repurchase from the firm.
- Percentage of customers who say they would recommend the firm to others.
- Percentage of customers who say that the company's products are the most preferred in its category.
- Percentage of customers who correctly identify the company's intended positioning and differentiation.
- Average perception of company's product quality relative to chief competitor.
- Average perception of company's service quality relative to chief competitor.

fulfillment, you can measure the percentage of "orders filled completely and accurately."

Every company must set appropriate incentives for the achievement of different goals. Companies must avoid setting incentives that create short-term profit but long-term customer loss. Paying automobile salespeople a commission leads them to manipulate the customer in order to make the sale. Stockbrokers on commission have an incentive to churn the customer's holdings. Insurance claims representatives try to pay as little as possible. Telemarketers are paid for speed over service and this can hurt long term relationship building. Incentive systems must be carefully monitored to avoid abuse.

Positioning

Thanks to Al Ries and Jack Trout, "positioning" entered the marketing vocabulary in 1982 when they wrote *Positioning: The Battle for Your Mind.*[47] Actually the word had been used earlier in connection with placing products in stores, hopefully at the eye-level position. However, Ries and Trout gave a new twist to the term: **"But positioning is not what you do to a product. Positioning is what you do to the mind of the prospect."** Thus Volvo tells us that it makes "the safest car"; BMW is "the ultimate driving machine"; and Porsche is "the world's best small sports car."

A company can claim to be different and better than another company in numerous ways: We are faster, safer, cheaper, more convenient, more durable, more friendly, higher quality, better value . . . the list goes on. But Ries and Trout emphasized the need to choose one of these so that it would stick in the buyer's mind. They saw positioning as primarily a communication exercise. Unless a product is identified as being best in some way that is meaningful to some set of customers, it will be poorly positioned and poorly remembered. We remember brands that stand out as first or best in some way.

But the positioning cannot be arbitrary. We wouldn't be able to get people to believe that Hyundai is "the ultimate driving machine." In fact, the product must be designed with an intended positioning in mind; the positioning must be decided before the product is designed. One of the tragic flaws in General Motors' car lineup is that it designs cars without distinctive positionings. After the car is made, GM struggles to decide how to position it.

Brands that are not number one in their market (measured by company size or some other attribute) don't have to worry—they simply need to select another attribute and be number one on that attribute. I consulted with a drug company that positioned its new drug as "fastest in relief." Its new competitor then positioned its brand as "safest." Each competitor will attract those customers who favor its major attribute.

Some companies prefer to build a multiple positioning instead of just a single positioning. The drug company could have called its drug the "fastest and safest drug on the market." But then another new competitor could co-opt the position "least expensive." Obviously, if a company claims too many superior attributes it won't be remembered or believed. Occasionally, however, this works, as when the toothpaste Aquafresh claimed that it offered a three-in-one benefit: fights cavities, whitens teeth, and gives cleaner breath.

Michael Treacy and Fred Wiersema distiguished among three major positionings (which they called "value disciplines"): *product leadership, operational excellence,* and *customer intimacy.*[48] Some customers value most the firm that offers the best product in the category; others value the firm that operates most efficiently; and still others value the firm that responds best to their wishes. They advise a firm to become the acknowledged leader in one of these value disciplines and be at least adequate in the other two. It would be too difficult or expensive for a company to be best in all three value disciplines.

Recently Fred Crawford and Ryan Mathews suggested five possible positionings: *product, price, ease of access, value-added service,* and *customer experience.*[49] Based on their study of successful companies, they concluded that a great company will *dominate* on one of these, perform above the average (*differentiate*) on a second, and be at *industry par* with respect to the remaining three. As an example, Wal-Mart dominates on price, differentiates on product (given its huge variety), and is average at ease of access, value-added service, and the customer experience. Crawford and Mathews hold that a company will suboptimize if it tries to be best in more than two ways.

The most successful positioning occurs with companies that have figured out how to be unique and very difficult to imitate. No one has successfully copied IKEA, Harley Davidson, Southwest Airlines, or Neutragena. These companies have developed hundreds of special processes for running their businesses. Their outer shells can be copied but not their inner workings.

Companies that lack a unique positioning can sometimes make a mark by resorting to the "number two" strategy. Avis is remembered for its motto: **"We're number two. We try harder."** And 7-Up is remembered for its **"Uncola"** strategy.

Alternatively, a company can claim to belonging to the exclusive club of the top performers in its industry: the Big Three auto firms, the Big Five accounting firms. They exploit the aura of being in the *leadership circle* that offers higher-quality products and services than those on the outside.

No positioning will work forever. As changes occur in consumers, competitors, technology, and the economy, companies must reevaluate the positioning of their major brands. Some brands that are losing share may need to be repositioned. This must be done carefully. Remaking your brand may win new customers but lose some current customers who like the brand as it is. If Volvo, for example, placed less emphasis on safety and more on slick styling, this could turn off practical-minded Volvo fans.

Price

Oscar Wilde saw a major difference between price and value: **"A cynic is a person who knows the price of everything and the value of nothing."** A businessman told me that his aim was to get a higher price for his product than was justified.

How much should you charge for your product? An old Russian proverb says: **"There are two fools in every market—one asks too little, another asks too much."**

Charging too little wins the sale but makes little profit. Furthermore, it attracts the wrong customers—those who will switch to save a dime. It also attracts competitors who will match or exceed the price cut. And it cheapens the customer's view of the product. Indeed, those who sell for less probably know what their stuff is worth.

Charging too much may lose both the sale and the customer. Peter Drucker adds another concern: **"The worship of premium prices always creates a market for a competitor."**

The standard approach to setting a price is to determine the cost and add a markup. But your cost has nothing to do with the customer's view of value. Your cost only helps you to know whether you should be making the product in the first place.

After you set the price, don't use the price to make the sale. You use the value to make the sale. As Lee Iacocca observed: **"When the product is right, you don't have to be a great marketer."** Jeff Bezos of Amazon said: **"I am not upset with someone who charges 5 percent less. I am concerned with someone who might offer a better experience."**

So how important is price? Christopher Fay of the Juran Institute said: **"In over 70 percent of businesses studied, price scored #1 or #2 as the feature with which customers are least satisfied. Yet among switchers, in no case were more than 10 percent motivated by price!"**

Globalization, hypercompetition, and the Internet are reshaping markets and businesses. All three forces act to increase downward pressure on prices. Globalization leads companies to move their production to cheaper sites and bring products into a country at prices lower than those charged by the domestic vendors. Hypercompetition amounts to more companies competing for the same customer, leading to price cuts. And the Internet allows people to more easily compare prices and move toward the lowest cost offer. The marketing challenge, then, is to find ways to maintain prices and profitability in the face of these macro trends.

The main answers seem to be better segmentation, stronger branding, and superior customer relationship management. These are discussed elsewhere in this book.

Products

Most companies define themselves by a product. We are a "car manufacturer," a "soft drink manufacturer," and so on. Theodore Levitt, former Harvard Business School faculty member, pointed out years ago the danger of focusing on the product and missing the underlying need. He accused the railroads of "marketing myopia" by failing to define themselves as being in the transportation business and overlooking the threat of trucks and airplanes. Steel companies did not pay enough attention to the impact of plastics and aluminum because they defined themselves as steel companies, not materials companies. Coca-Cola missed the development of fruit-flavored drinks, health and energy drinks, and even bottled water by overfocusing on the soft drink category.

How do companies decide what to sell? There are four paths:

1. Selling something that already exists.
2. Making something that someone asks for.
3. Anticipating something that someone will ask for.
4. Making something that no one asked for but that will give buyers great delight.

The last path involves much higher risk but the chance of much higher gain.

Don't just sell a product. Sell an experience. Harley Davidson sells more than a motorcycle. It sells an ownership experience. It delivers membership in a community. It arranges adventure tours. It sells a lifestyle. The *total product* far exceeds the motorcycle.

And help the buyer use the product. Explain how it works, how it can be used safely, how its life can be extended. If I pay $30,000 for a car, I would like to buy it from a company that helps me stretch the most value from its use. Carl Sewell preached this message in his book (with Paul Brown), *Customers for Life*.[50] He not only sold cars, but assumed responsibility for fixing them, cleaning them, offering loaners, and so on.

It costs more to build and sell bad products than good products. The late Bruce Henderson, who was head of the Boston Consulting Group, noted: **"The majority of the products in most companies are cash traps. . . . They are not only worthless but a perpetual drain on corporate resources."** In slow economies in particular, companies need to concentrate their investments in a smaller group of power brands that command a price premium, high loyalty, and a leading market share, and are stretchable into related categories. Unilever decided to prune its 1,600 brands and focus its huge advertising and promotion budget on 400 power brands.

Too many companies carry a poorly constructed product portfolio. My advice is that your company must participate in several parts of any market that it wants to dominate. Marriott's major role in the hotel marketplace is based on its use of different price brands from Fairmont to Courtyard to Marriott to Ritz-Carlton. And Kraft conquered the frozen pizza market by creating four brands: Jack's aims at the low-price end; Original Tombstone competes with the midprice frozen brands; DiGiorno's competes in quality with freshly delivered pizzas; and California Pizza Kitchen aims at the high end, charging three times the price per pound of the lower-end offerings.

At the same time, it is not always the best product that wins the market. Many users regard Apple's Macintosh software as better than Microsoft's software, but Microsoft owns the market. And Sony's Betamax offered better recording quality than Matsushita's VHS, but VHS won. Sometimes it is the better marketed product, not the better product, that wins. Professor Theodore Levitt of Harvard observed: **"A product is not a product unless it sells. Otherwise it is merely a museum piece."**

Profits

Should a company aim at maximizing current profits? No! Companies formerly thought that they would make the most profit by paying the least to their suppliers, employees, distributors, and dealers. This is *zero-sum thinking*, namely that there is a fixed pie and the company keeps the most by giving its partners the least. This is a fallacy; the company ends up attracting poor suppliers, poor employees, and poor distributors. Their outputs are poor, they are demoralized, many leave, replacement costs are high, and the company is impoverished.

Today's winning companies work on the *positive-sum theory of marketing*. They contract with excellent suppliers, employees, distributors, and dealers. They operate together as a team seeking a win-win-win outcome. And the company ends up as a stronger winner.

A company that is short-run profit driven will not make long-run profits. The Navajo Indians are smarter. A Navajo chief does not make a decision unless he has considered its possible effects on seven generations hence.

Some companies hope to increase profits by cutting costs. But as Gary Hamel observed: **"Excessive downsizing and cost cutting is a type of corporate anorexia . . . getting thin all right, but not very healthy."** You can't shrink to greatness.

Here's the story of one company that thought that its profits lay in cost cutting.

> The company, a manufacturer of hospital devices, suffered from flat sales and profits. The CEO was intent on improving the company's profits and share price. So he ordered across-the-board cost cuts. Profits rose, and he waited for the stock price to rise as well. When it didn't, he went to Wall Street to find out why. The analysts told him that his bottom line had improved but not his top line—they didn't see any revenue growth. So the CEO decided to cut product prices to increase top line growth. He succeeded, but the bottom line now slipped. The moral: Investors favor companies that can increase both their growth (top line) and their profitability (bottom line).

Ram Charan and Noel M. Tichy believe companies can achieve growth and profitability together, and present that view in their *Every Business Is a Growth Business: How Your Company Can Prosper Year after Year*.[51] This is a bold claim, given that top management always faces trade-offs. But they make a compelling case.

Some companies have proven that they can charge low prices and be highly profitable. Car rental firm Enterprise has the lowest prices and makes the most profit in its industry. This can also be said of Southwest Airlines, Wal-Mart, and Dell.

To understand the source of the profits of these "low price" companies, recognize that *return* (R) is the product of *margin × velocity*; that is:

$$R = \frac{\text{Income}}{\text{Sales}} \times \frac{\text{Sales}}{\text{Assets}}$$

A low-price firm makes less income on its sales (because its price is lower) but generates considerably more sales per dollar of assets (because more customers are attracted by its lower price). This works when the low-price firm gives good quality and service to its customers.

Profits come from finding ways to deliver more value to customers. Peter Drucker admonished: **"Customers do not see it as their job to ensure manufacturers a profit."** Companies have to figure out not only how to increase sales but how to earn customers' repeat business. The most profit comes from repeat sales.

At board meetings, the talk focuses primarily on current profit performance. But the company's true performance goes beyond the financial numbers. Jerre L. Stead, chairman and CEO of NCR, understood this: **"I say if you're in a meeting, any meeting, for 15 minutes, and we're not talking about customers or competitors, raise your hand and ask why."**

Here are four Japanese-formulated objectives for achieving exceptional profitability. Each deserves a textbook-size discussion:

1. *Zero customer feedback time.* Learning from customer reactions as soon as possible.
2. *Zero product improvement time.* Continuously improving the product and service.

3. *Zero inventory.* Carrying as little inventory as possible.
4. *Zero defects.* Producing products and services with no defects.

Too many companies spend more time measuring product profitability than customer profitability. But the latter is more important. **"The only profit center is the customer."** (Peter Drucker)

Public Relations

I expect companies to start shifting more money from advertising to public relations. Advertising is losing some of its former effectiveness. It is hard to reach a mass audience because of increasing audience fragmentation. TV commercials are getting shorter; they are bunched together; they are increasingly undistinguished; and consumers are zapping them. And the biggest problem is that advertising lacks credibility. The public knows that advertising exaggerates and is biased. At its best, advertising is playful and entertaining; at its worst, it is intrusive and dishonest.

Companies overspend on advertising and underspend on public relations. The reason: Nine out of 10 PR agencies are owned by advertising firms. Advertising agencies make more money putting out ads than putting out PR. So they don't want PR to get an upper hand.

Ad campaigns do have the advantage of being under greater

control than PR. The media are purchased for the ads to appear at specific times; the ads are approved by the client and will appear exactly as designed. PR, on the other hand, is something you pray for rather than pay for. You hope that when Oprah Winfrey ran her book club, she would nominate your book as the month's best read; you hope that Morley Safer will run a *60 Minutes* segment on why red wine keeps cheese-eating and oil-eating Europeans healthy.

Building a new brand through PR takes much more time and creativity, but it ultimately can do a better job than "big bang" advertising. Public relations consists of a whole bag of tools for grabbing attention and creating "talk value." I call these tools the *PENCILS* of public relations:

- *P*ublications.
- *E*vents.
- *N*ews.
- *C*ommunity affairs.
- *I*dentity media.
- *L*obbying.
- *S*ocial investments.

Most of us got to hear about Palm, Amazon, eBay, The Body Shop, Blackberry, Beanie Babies, Viagra, and Nokia not through advertising but through news stories in print and on the air. We started to hear from friends about these products, and we told other friends. And hearing from others about a product carries much more weight than reading about the product in an ad.

A company planning to build a new brand needs to create a buzz, and the buzz is created through PR tools. The PR campaign will cost much less and hopefully create a more lasting story. Al and Laura Ries, in their book *The Fall of Advertising and the Rise of PR*, argue persuasively that in launching a new product, it is better to start with public relations, not advertising.[52] This is the reverse of most companies' thinking when they launch new products.

Quality

It continues to amaze me how many Americans accepted bad quality in the past. When I took my newly purchased Buick to the dealer one week after purchasing it, he said: "You're lucky. We have only one repair to make."

General Motors' theory of wealth creation ran as follows: Produce as many cars as you can in the factory. Don't fix them there. Send them to the dealer and let the dealer fix them. There was no thought about the cost to the customer who had to drive back to the dealer, give up the car, and pray that he or she could find alternative transportation while the car was being fixed.

Who was responsible for poor quality? Management blamed the workers. But the workers were not responsible. The great quality expert W. Edwards Deming declared: **"Management is responsible for 85% of quality problems."**

The Japanese are sticklers for high quality. When they detect a defect, they ask the five Why's. "Why was there a tear in the leather seat?" "Why was the leather not inspected when it arrived in our factory?" "Why didn't the supplier detect the tear before sending the leather to us?" "Why is the supplier's machine lacking a laser reader?" "Why is the supplier not buying better equipment?" These questions aim to get at the root cause of a defect so that it won't happen again.

How high should the quality be? In making computer chips, Motorola aims for a six sigma quality level so that there will be no more than three or four defects per million chips. This is much higher quality than is needed if the chips are used in cheap radios; and this is lower than one would want in chips guiding 747s. The right quality level depends on the customer and the product.

Brendan Power, motivational speaker, says: **"Our customers set our quality standards. Our job is to meet them."** Peter Drucker also sees quality coming from the customer: **"Quality in a service or product is not what you put into it. It is what the client or customer gets out of it."** Electronics giant Siemens has the quality motto: **"Quality is when our customers come back and our products don't."**

GE's Jack Welch ably summed up the importance of quality: **"Quality is our best assurance of customer allegiance, our strongest defense against foreign competition, and the only path to sustained growth and earnings."**

The lesson: Cheap quality is expensive; good quality is cheap.

Recession Marketing

When a recession strikes, most companies rush to cut their expenses, the most obvious one being advertising. Those in top management (mostly finance guys) don't believe in advertising, anyway; they tolerate it as a form of defensive insurance, not as a profit generator. They have set the whole marketing budget as a percentage of expected revenue, and when expected revenue drops, they see every reason to cut marketing expenditures. But this exposes the illogic of setting marketing expenditures based on expected revenue. This is putting the cart before the horse. One doesn't know expected revenue except by setting the marketing budget. The marketing budget is the cause, not the effect. Set a higher marketing budget and you will get a higher expected revenue.

Kmart's CEO decided to cut Kmart's marketing budget when the recession struck. The result was disastrous, and Kmart lost far more in sales than it had saved in marketing costs as customers moved their business to Target and Wal-Mart.

When a recession appears imminent, the CEO should appoint a multifunctional committee to propose what the company should do to reduce costs. The committee should examine the company's promotion mix, channel mix, market segment mix, customer mix, and geographic mix for activities and expenses that can safely be reduced. Every company has some losing or weak promotions, channels, market segments, customers, and geographic areas. A recession calls for housecleaning.

The basic problem is that in good times companies develop a lot of *organizational fat.* They buy excessively expensive furniture, pay for high-priced country club memberships, acquire company aircraft, hire a lot of consultants, and say good-bye to thrift. Then they painfully lay off a large number of workers when the recession strikes.

Companies can save money by switching their salespeople to economy-class flights and hotels. They can try to renegotiate purchasing contracts. They can delay selected long-term R&D projects and postpone capital projects. They can try to speed up collections and slow down payments.

During a recession, many companies rush to impose cost-cutting measures. But whatever measures they take, they should observe two rules. First, don't compromise your *customer value proposition.* Customers buy from you with a certain set of expectations about product quality and service. Don't reduce the experience that they have come to expect. Second, don't arbitrarily shift the cost burden to your suppliers and dealers without consultation. If you hurt your *partner value proposition*, partners will start shifting their alliances to your competitors.

Companies should consider temporarily lowering their prices, even though this will hurt their margins. It is better to hold on to your customers than to let them switch and sample your competitors. Because customers are highly price sensitive during a recession, price concessions are warranted.

Some smart companies, instead of resorting to cost cutting, may maintain or increase their budgets to grab market share from competitors who are reducing their budgets. If a company has the resources, it may see the recession as an opportunity to grow its business at the expense of its competitors. One study found that companies that maintained their marketing spending during the recession emerged stronger after the recession that those that didn't.[53]

Even smarter companies will build a cost-conscious culture not just when recession strikes but all the time. Winnebago Industries, the leading manufacturer of recreational vehicles in the United States, has built frugality into the heart of its culture. Every week Cost Savings Award checks are handed out for cost-saving suggestions. Because Winnebago practices *lean business* all the time, only minor surgery is called for when recession strikes.

Relationship Marketing

One of the things of most value to a company is its relationships— with customers, employees, suppliers, distributors, dealers, and retailers. The company's *relationship capital* is the sum of the knowledge, experience, and trust a company has with its customers, employees, suppliers, and distribution partners. These relationships are often worth more than the physical assets of a company. Relationships determine the future value of the firm.

Any slips in these relationships will hurt the company's performance. Companies need to keep a *relationship scorecard* that describes the strengths, weaknesses, opportunities, and threats in regard to the relationship. Your company needs to move fast and repair any important but weakening relationships.

Traditional transaction marketing (TM) tended to ignore relationships and relationship building. The company was viewed as an independent agency always maneuvering to secure the best terms. The company was ready to switch from one supplier or distributor to another if there was an immediate advantage. The company assumed that it would normally keep its current customers, and it spent most of its energy to acquire new customers. The company neglected the interdependence among its main stakeholders and their roles in affecting the company's success.

Relationship marketing (RM) marks a significant paradigm shift in marketing, a movement from thinking solely in terms of competition and conflict toward thinking in terms of mutual interdependence and cooperation. It recognizes the importance of various parties—suppliers, employees, distributors, dealers, retailers—cooperating to deliver the best value to the target customers. Here are the main characteristics of relationship marketing:

- It focuses on partners and customers rather than on the company's products.
- It puts more emphasis on customer retention and growth than on customer acquisition.
- It relies on cross-functional teams rather than on departmental-level work.
- It relies more on listening and learning than on talking.

Relationship marketing calls for new practices within the 4Ps (see box).

The shift toward relationship marketing does not mean that companies abandon transaction marketing altogether. Most companies need to operate with a mixture of the transactional and

Relationship Marketing and the 4Ps

Product
- More products are customized to the customers' preferences.
- New products are developed and designed cooperatively with suppliers and distributors.

Price
- The company will set a price based on the relationship with the customer and the bundle of features and services ordered by the customer.
- In business-to-business marketing, there is more negotiation because products are often designed for each customer.

Distribution
- RM favors more direct marketing to the customer, thus reducing the role of middlemen.
- RM favors offering alternatives to customers to choose the way they want to order, pay for, receive, install, and even repair the product.

Communication
- RM favors more individual communication and dialogue with customers.
- RM favors more integrated marketing communications to deliver the same promise and image to the customer.
- RM sets up extranets with large customers to facilitate information exchange, joint planning, ordering, and payments.

the relational marketing approaches. Companies selling in large consumer markets practice a greater percentage of TM while companies with a smaller number of customers practice a higher percentage of RM.

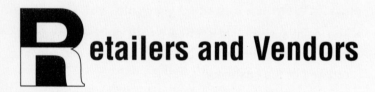

Retailers and Vendors

When retailers were small, manufacturers had the power. The strongest manufacturers could dictate the terms and shelf space they wanted for their products. The advent of giant retailers—hypermarkets, superstores, category killers—changed the power forever. No longer were the retailers the dumping grounds for the manufacturers' products; instead they became the customers' representatives. The retailers chose to carry the goods that would most satisfy their customers. And the giant retailers ordered such high volume that they could play off the manufacturers against each other for the best terms. A company such as Toys 'R' Us commanded such a significant share of the toy market that it insisted on participating even in the design and packaging of new toys that it would consider carrying.

The shift of power from manufacturers to retailers is vividly captured by Bowling Green sales manager Kevin Price's remark: **"A decade ago, the retailer was a chihuahua nipping at the** manufacturer's heels—a nuisance, yes, but only a minor irritant; you fed it and it went away. Today it's a pit bull and it wants to rip your arms and legs off. You'd like to see it roll over, but you're too busy defending yourself to even try."[54]

The only force taming giant retailers is the competition they face from other giant retailers: Home Depot vs. Lowe's; Sam's vs. Costco; Barnes & Noble vs. Borders; Office Max vs. Office Depot vs. Staples; Circuit City vs. Best Buy.

Retail is detail. It is hard work. Cyril Magnin, an American merchant, advised: **"If you are over 40 years old, you don't belong in retailing."** An old Chinese proverb adds this advice: **"If you cannot smile, do not open a shop."**

The three success factors in retailing used to be "location, location, location." With the advent of the Internet, physical location is less important. Millions of people buy books from Amazon.com without knowing the company's physical location. All that is needed is an Internet address.

Companies need to solidify their relationships with their vendors. A company should form a vendor council that meets a few times a year. The vendors should be encouraged to critique the company's performance and make suggestions. The company needs to send its experts to visit and help vendors improve their business practices. The company should learn from its best vendors and inform other vendors of *best practices*. And the top-performing vendors deserve recognition and better terms.

Today's retailers must adopt new practices to survive in the brutal marketplace. First, retailers need to spend more time in learning who their customers are. They should give their customers a club card and capture information in their customer databases. By analyzing customer purchases, they will know which ones buy a lot of wine or fish or ice cream, and can then announce and run special events for these customer segments.

Second, retailers must invest in making retailing an experience rather than a chore. Brand experience counts for much more than brand image. By designing a distinctive brand experience, store owners encourage people to come back more often, as has been demonstrated by Barnes & Noble, Stew Leonard's supermarket, and other top retailers.

Third, retailers must move more aggressively into private branding. Private brands make more money for retailers than national brands. At one time, store brands were considered inferior to national brands. Then along came President's Choice introduced by Canada's Loblaws supermarkets, a store brand that exceeded the quality of some national brands. The next step was for retailers to carry two or three store brands pitched at different quality and price levels. The main requirement was to create trust in the retailer and to give good value to the customer.

Fourth, a retailer should open up a web site and offer customers more information and opportunity for contact and dialogue.

Sales Force

About 11 percent of all employed people, or 18 million people, are engaged in selling. The emergence of the Internet and other direct marketing techniques, along with the high cost of personal selling, is leading companies to reexamine the size and role of their sales forces.

Are salespeople necessary? According to Peter Drucker: **"People are simply too expensive to be used for selling. We cannot, by and large, sell anymore—we must market, i.e., we must create the desire to buy which we then can satisfy without a great deal of selling."**

Companies don't always need their own sales forces. About 50 percent of companies use contract sales forces: manufacturers' reps, sales agents, and so on. Many companies hire outside salespeople to handle more marginal geographical areas and market segments.

In hiring salespeople, you should hire only those who are sold on the company and its products. This is hard to fake. And you might prefer people who have failed, rather than those who never tried. And don't hire any salesperson whom you wouldn't want to invite to your home for dinner.

In deciding on how much to pay salespeople, remember that low-paid salespeople are expensive, and high-paid salespeople are cheap. Top salespeople in a company often sell five times as much as the average salesperson but don't get paid five times as much.

Salespeople need to be motivated, much like football players huddled in a locker room. The real talent is to be able to motivate the average salesperson, not just the star performers.

Watch out for the salesperson who thinks any sale is good no matter what its profitability. Tie compensation to the profit on the sale, not to the revenue. Each salesperson should see himself or herself as managing a profit center, not a sales center, and be rewarded accordingly.

Here are other measures to look at in judging a salesperson's performance: *average number of sales calls per day, average sales-call time per contact, average cost and revenue per sales call, percentage of orders per hundred sales calls,* and *number of new and lost customers per sales period.* Then compare this salesperson's performance to the average salesperson's performance to detect poor or exceptionally good performance.

Poor performance is often excused by saying the market is mature. But calling a market "mature" is evidence of incompetence. It is probably easier to make money in a mature industry than in a high-tech industry, to take an extreme case.

The hardest job facing a salesperson is to tell a customer that a competitor has the better product. IBM expects its sales reps to recommend the best equipment for an application, even if this means recommending a competitor's hardware. But the sales rep will win the customer's respect and eventually his or her business.

Marketing's role is to support the sales force in the following ways:

- Marketing places ads and buys lists to identify new prospects.
- Marketing prepares a profile of the best prospects so that salespeople know who to call on and who not to call on.
- Marketing describes the buying influences and rationales used by key customer decision makers.

- Marketing highlights competitors' strengths and weaknesses and how the company's products rate against competitors' offerings.
- Marketing documents and distributes sales success stories and uses them in training programs.
- Marketing prepares and distributes communications (advertising, brochures, etc.) to customers to stimulate interest in the company's products and make salespeople more welcome.
- Marketing uses advertising and telemarketing to find and qualify leads that can be turned over to the sales force.

Smart companies are equipping their salespeople with sales automation equipment (computers, cell phones, fax and copy machines) and software. Salespeople can research the customer before the visit, answer questions during the visit, and record important facts after the visit. Salespeople can retrieve product information such as tech bulletins, pricing information, customer buying history, preferred payment terms, and other data to facilitate their work.

When the salesperson finally makes the sale, **"The salesmen's anxiety ends and the customer's anxiety begins."** (Theodore Levitt)

Sales Promotion

Sales promotion describes incentives and rewards to get customers to buy now rather than later. Whereas advertising is a long-run tool for shaping the market's attitude toward a brand, sales promotion is a short-term tool to trigger buyer action. No wonder brand managers increasingly rely on sales promotion, especially when falling behind in achieving sales quotas. Sales promotions work! Sales promotions yield faster and more measurable responses in sales than advertising does. Today the split between advertising and sales promotion may be 30–70, the reverse of what it used to be.

The growth of sales promotion reflects the higher priority companies are attaching to current sales than to long-term brand building. It is a return to transaction marketing (TM) rather than relationship marketing (RM).

Sales promotion can be directed at retailers, consumers, and the sales force. Retailers will work harder if offered price-offs, advertising and display allowances, and free goods. Consumers are more likely to buy in response to coupons, rebates, price packs, premiums, patronage awards, contests, product demonstrations, and warranties. The sales force operates more vigorously in response to contests with prizes for superior performance.

Because of the variety of sales promotion tools, marketers need experience in knowing which to use. Some large companies have a sales promotion specialist who can advise brand managers. Or the company can engage the services of a specialist sales promotion agency. The main need is to not only use promotions but to review and record results so that the company can improve its sales promotion efficiency over time.

Although most sales promotions increase sales, most lose money. One analyst estimated that only 17 percent of a given set of sales promotion campaigns were profitable. These are the cases where the sales promotion brings in new customers to sample the product and where they like the new product better than their previous brand. But many sales promotions only attract brand switchers looking for a lower price, who naturally abandon the brand when another brand goes on sale. Sales promotions are less likely to entice away loyal users of other brands.

Thus sales promotions work poorest in product markets of high brand similarity. They tend to attract brand switchers who are looking for low price or premiums and who won't be loyal to a brand. It is better to use sales promotions in product markets of high dissimilarity where new customers may find that they like your product and its features better than their previous choice.

Sales promotions tend to be used more by weaker and smaller brands than stronger brands. Smaller brands have fewer funds to spend on advertising, and for a small cost they can get people to at least try their product.

Sales promotions in general should be used sparingly. Incessant prices off, coupons, deals, and premiums can devalue the brand in the consumers' minds. They can lead customers to wait for the next promotion instead of buying now.

Companies are forced to use more sales promotion than they want by the trade. The trade demands discounts and allowances as a condition for putting the product on the shelf. The trade may demand consumer promotions also. So many companies have little choice but to comply.

Prefer sales promotions that agree or enhance your brand image and add value. Try to use sales promotions *with* advertising. Advertising explains why the customer should buy the product, and sales promotion provides the incentive to buy. When used together, ads and sales promotions make a powerful combination.

Segmentation

In the past, companies such as Sears or Coca-Cola, when asked who their customer is, would answer "Everybody." But a marketer can rarely satisfy everyone in a market. Not everyone will like the same camera, car, cafeteria, or concert. Therefore, marketers must start by dividing up the market.

Companies that moved away from mass market thinking started by identifying large *market segments*. Procter & Gamble, in selling its Duncan Hines cake mix, would define the target market as "married women between the ages of 35 and 50 with families." Later companies moved from large segments to *narrower niches*. Estée Lauder might design a product for "black American professional women between the ages of 25 and 35." Finally, some companies have moved to the ultimate segmentation scheme, *segments of one*, namely individual customers.

Today more companies are guilty of undersegmentation than oversegmentation. They imagine more high-potential prospects for their offerings than really exist. The antidote is to divide the market into several levels of potential. The first level consists of those customers who would be the most responsive to the offering. This group should be profiled in terms of their demographic and psychographic characteristics. Then a secondary group and a tertiary group should be defined. The company should then focus its initial selling on its primary prospects; if they don't respond, the company either has mis-segmented or its offering is of little interest.

Segments can be identified in three ways. The traditional approach is to divide the market into *demographic groups*, such as "women between the ages of 35 and 50." This has the advantage of ease of reaching this group. Its disadvantage is that there is no reason to believe that women in this group have similar needs or readiness to buy. Demographic segmentation is more about identifying a population *sector* than a population *segment*.

The second approach is to segment the market into *need groups*, such as "women who want to save time in shopping for food." This is a clear need that can be met by a number of solutions, such as a supermarket taking telephone orders or Web orders that would be delivered to the home. The hope would be to identify demographic or psychographic characteristics of such women, such as being more highly educated or having a higher income.

The third approach is to segment the market by *behavior groups*, such as "women who order their food from Peapod and other home delivery groups." This group is defined by their actual behavior, not just needs, and the analyst can then search for common characteristics that they may have.

Once you identify a distinct segment, the question is whether it should be managed within the existing organization or deserves to be set up as a separate business. In the latter case, Nirmalya Kumar calls it a *strategic segment*. For example, food companies such as Kraft and Unilever focus primarily on their retail sales and only secondarily on food service systems. But food service requires different quantities, packages, and selling systems. It is a strategic segment and should be run independently of the food retailing group and manage its own strategy and requirements.

 **S** **elling**

"Everyone lives by selling something," noted the novelist Robert Louis Stevenson. People are selling either a product, a service, a place, an idea, information, or themselves.

Cynics view selling is a form of civilized warfare fought with words, ideas, and disciplined thinking. And they view marketing as an effort to add an element of dignity to what is otherwise a vulgar brawl.

There are many images of selling. The YTS school says that selling consists of "yell, tell, and sell." The S&P school says selling is "spray and pray," The LGD school says that selling is "lunch, golf, and dinner." And the salesperson is described as a "talking brochure."

There is the well-known story of the Stanley Works in which a consultant told the tool company, "You are not in the business of selling drills. You are in the business of selling holes." Don't sell features. Sell benefits, outcomes, and value.

Some individuals are gifted salespeople. They can sell refrigerators to Eskimos, fur coats to Hawaiians, sand to Arabs, all at a profit, and then repurchase them at a discount.

Good salespeople remember that they are born with two ears and one mouth. This reminds them that they should be doing twice as much listening as talking. If you want to lose the sale, make a pitch to the customer.

Some salespeople can be painful bores. Woody Allen lamented: **"There are worse things in life than death. Have you ever spent an evening with an insurance salesman?"**

Salespeople must get used to being rejected. Dennis Tamcsin of Northwestern Mutual Life Insurance observed: **"We have something in this industry called the 10-3-1 ratio. This means that for every 10 calls a salesperson makes, he will only get to make a presentation to three, and if he's got a good success rate, he'll make one sale. We need people who won't shrink from that kind of rejection."**

IBM trains its salespeople to act as if they are always on the verge of losing every customer.

What makes a successful salesperson? To succeed, a salesperson must recognize that the first person he or she has to sell to is himself or herself. His job is to get in touch with the buyer within himself. And his motto should be: "I develop clients, not sales."

The comedian George Burns had his own opinion about what makes a successful salesperson: **"The most important thing in relationship selling is honesty and integrity. If you can fake them, you've got it made."**

Here is a story that illustrates the difference between great salespeople and average salespeople.

A Hong Kong shoe manufacturer wondered whether a market existed for his shoes on a remote South Pacific island. He sent an *order taker* to the island who, upon a cursory examination, wired back: "The people here do not wear shoes. There is no market." Not convinced, the Hong Kong manufacturer sent a *salesperson* to the island. This salesperson wired back: "The people here don't wear shoes. There is a tremendous market." Afraid that this salesrep was being carried away by the sight of so many shoeless feet, the manufacturer sent a third person, a *marketer*. This marketing professional interviewed the tribal chief and several natives and wired back:

"The people here don't wear shoes. As a result their feet are sore and bruised. I have shown the chief how shoes would help his people avoid foot problems. He is enthusiastic. He estimates the 70 percent of his people will buy the shoes at $10 a pair. We probably can sell 5,000 pairs of shoes in the first year. Our cost of bringing the shoes to the island and setting up distribution would amount to $6 a pair. We will clear $20,000 in the first year, which, given our investment, will give us a rate of return on our investment (ROI) of 20 percent, which exceeds our normal ROI of 15 percent. This is not to mention the high value of our future earnings by entering this market. I recommend that we go ahead."

This illustrates that effective marketing involves careful research into the market opportunity and the preparation of financial estimates based on the proposed strategy indicating whether the returns would meet or exceed the company's financial objectives.

In the past, a gifted salesperson was one who could "communicate value." But as products have become more similar, each competitive salesperson delivers essentially the same message. So the new need is for the salesperson who can "create value" by helping the customer make or save more money. Salespeople must move from persuading to consulting. This can take the form of providing technical help, solving a difficult problem for the customer, or even helping the customer change its whole way of doing business.

Service

In an age of increasing product commoditization, service quality is one of the most promising sources of differentiation and distinction. Giving good service is the essence of practicing a customer orientation.

Yet many companies view service as a pain, a cost, as something to minimize. Companies rarely make it easy for customers to make inquiries, submit suggestions, or lodge complaints. They see providing service as a duty and an overhead, not as an opportunity and a marketing tool.

Every business is a service business. You are not a chemical company. You are a chemical services business. Theodore Levitt said: **"There is no such things as service industries. There are** only industries whose service components are greater or less than those of other industries. Everybody is in service."

"Businesses planned for service are apt to succeed; businesses planned for profit are apt to fail," observed American educator Nicholas Murray Butler.

What service level should a company deliver? Good service is not enough. Nobody talks about good service. Sam Walton, founder of Wal-Mart, set a higher goal: "Our goal as a company is to have customer service that is not just the best, but legendary." The three Fs of service marketing are be fast, flexible, and friendly.

What is poor service? There are stories that tell of a hotel in Spain that advertises that it will accept service complaints at the front desk only from 9 to 11 A.M. each day. And there is a store in England whose sign reads, "We offer quality, service, and low price. Choose any two."

There are two ways to get a service reputation: One is to be the best at service; the other is to be the worst at service.

Ellsworth Statler, who founded the Statler hotels, trained his people with the dictum: "In all minor discussions between Statler employees and Statler guests, the employee is dead wrong."

You can check on the service quality of your organization by becoming a customer for a day. Phone your company as if you are a customer and put some questions to the employee. Go into one of your stores and try to buy your product. Call about returning a product or complaining about it and see how the employee handles it. You are bound to be disappointed.

Check the *smile index* of your employees. Remember, "A smile is the shortest distance between two people." (Victor Borge)

Sponsorship

Companies are constantly invited by various groups to sponsor events, activities, and worthwhile causes. Companies also actively seek venues where they can get their names before the public. For example, Coca-Cola has been a long-term participating sponsor of Olympic Games, World Cups, Super Bowls, and Academy Awards. By shelling out large sums of money, Coca-Cola hopes to gain favorable public attention and also treat its associates to big-time *events*.

Companies will put out good money to place their names on *physical facilities* such as buildings, universities, and stadiums to keep their names in the public's eye. Sometimes this backfires; Houston had to find a new name for Enron Field.

Companies can sponsor an important *cause* (such as better eating, more exercise, regular doctor appointments, saying no to drugs) in what is called "cause-related marketing." By partnering with a cause that many people believe in, the company can enhance its corporate reputation, raise brand awareness, increase customer loyalty, build sales, and increase favorable press coverage.[55]

Companies are increasingly borrowing the auras of *celebrities* to add radiance to their own names. Celebrities bring high attention to the brand, add to its credibility, and offer reassurance. Not surprisingly,

169

singers, actors, and sports figures stand ready to sell their auras. Reebok has acquired the aura of Venus Williams ($40 million contract) and Nike has acquired Tiger Woods' aura ($100 million contract).

But be careful. PepsiCo borrowed the auras of Michael Jackson, Mike Tyson, and Madonna, all of which backfired. And Hertz borrowed O. J. Simpson's aura, only to regret it.

Sponsorship can turn out to be either an expense or an investment. If the money doesn't generate increased sales or corporate equity, then it is an expense. Companies that want to make the expenditure an investment have to be much more careful in deciding what to sponsor.

The question is what does a company gain from putting its name on a stadium, a Formula One racing car, a golf tournament, or an art show? Does it help the company sell more stuff? Most companies haven't really thought through their sponsorships. In fact, they often start a sponsorship that they continue indefinitely because of inertia or from their fear of being criticized for dropping the sponsorship.

If your company is going to sponsor something, make sure that it is a reasonable and relevant match to your target market and type of product/service. A good example is Timex's sponsorship of the Ironman Triathlon to convey that its watches "take a licking and keep on ticking." On the other hand, it wouldn't make sense for Nestlé's baby food division to sponsor a nursing home event.

Make sure that you decide on the objectives you are trying to achieve with the sponsorship. The money must have a positive impact on awareness, image, or customer loyalty that somehow turns into more sales. Ask how much your sales will have to increase to justify the cost. After each sponsorship, do a postaudit of whether it achieves the objectives. Granted, it is difficult to measure the value a company receives from many of its sponsorship dollars. If you find that it didn't contribute much value, write it off as philanthropy.[56]

trategy

Strategy is the glue that aims to build and deliver a consistent and distinctive value proposition to your target market. Bruce Henderson, founder of the Boston Consulting Group, warned: **"Unless a business has a unique advantage over its rivals, it has no reason to exist."**

If you have the same strategy as your competitors, you don't have a strategy. If the strategy is different, but easily copied, it is a weak strategy. If the strategy is uniquely different and difficult to copy, you have a strong and sustainable strategy.

Harvard's Michael Porter drew a clear distinction between operational excellence and strategic positioning.[57] Too many companies think they have a strategy by pursuing operational excellence. They work hard at "benchmarking" the "best-of-class performers" to stay ahead of their competition. But if they are running the same race as their competitors, their competitors may catch up. Their real need is to run a different race. Companies that target a specific group of customers and needs and deliver a different bundle of benefits can be said to have a strategy.

Several companies can be cited as having distinctive strategies.

171

- Southwest Airlines, the most profitable U.S. airline, is run differently than other airlines in dozens of ways: It targets price-sensitive, short-trip passengers; it flies point-to-point rather than through hubs; it uses only 737s, thus reducing spare parts inventory and pilot training costs; it sells only economy class and doesn't give seat assignments; it doesn't serve food; it doesn't move baggage to other carriers; and so on. The net results are that Southwest can take off after landing in 20 minutes compared to the average of 60 minutes for competitors, and its equipment is in the air longer and yields a higher return on its investment.
- IKEA, the world's largest furniture retailer, searches for low-cost real estate in a major city, builds a giant store with a restaurant and day care center, sells good quality furniture at a lower price that customers take home in their cars and put together, offers membership privileges leading to even lower prices, and in a dozen ways remains hard to copy by any would-be imitators.
- Harley Davidson not only sells motorcycles but provides entry into a social community that rides together, has races, and shares the Harley Davidson lifestyle with its HD leather jackets and clothing, watches, pens, watches, and restaurants.

Companies have a unique strategy when (1) they have defined a clear target market and need, (2) developed a distinctive and winning value proposition for that market, and (3) arranged a distinctive supply network to deliver the value proposition to the target market. Nirmalya Kumar calls this the 3Vs: *value target*, *value proposition*, and *value network*. Such companies cannot easily be copied because of the unique fit of their business processes and activities.

Companies that forge a unique way of doing business gain lower costs, higher prices, or both. While their competitors increasingly resemble each other and are forced to compete on price, strategically positioned companies avoid the bloodbath by following the beat of a different drummer.

Looking at strategy this way prevents companies from thinking they have a strategy because they are going on the Internet, or outsourcing, or restructuring, or acquiring other firms, or adopting customer relationship management. These business initiatives can easily be copied. They don't define how a business is going about building a sustainable strategy.

One of the best rules for strategy development is to strive to find out what the target customers like and do more of it; and find out what they dislike and do less of it. This means spending time in the marketplace and seeing what matters. As stated by Al Ries and Jack Trout, **"Strategy should evolve out of the mud of the marketplace, not in the antiseptic environment of an ivory tower."**

Your strategy should be some unique synthesis of features, design, quality, service, and cost. You have succeeded in building an enviable strategy when it has created such an advantageous market position that competition can only retaliate over a long time period and at a prohibitive cost.

What is bad strategy? We know it when we see it.

- *Yesterday's strategy.* Sears and GM, for example, tend to be responsive to the marketplace of yesterday. **"You can't have a better tomorrow if you are thinking about yesterday all the time."** (Charles F. Kettering, American inventor) In too many companies, the old strategy is "baked in." Dee Hock, CEO emeritus of Visa, said: **"The problem is never how to get new innovative thoughts into the mind, but how to get the old ones out."**
- *Protectionism.* American steel companies lack strategy because they spend their time urging protectionism. Protectionism is a sure way to lose your business.

- *Marketing shootouts.* Price wars and mutual destruction indicate the absence of strategy rather than its presence.
- *Overfocusing on problems.* Peter Drucker warned against **"feeding problems while starving opportunities."**
- *Lack of clear objectives.* Companies often fail to spell out or prioritize their objectives. **"If you don't know where you're going, it's really hard to get there."** (Viri Mullins, president, Armstrong's Lock & Supply). I have a strong bias toward advising a company to do what is strategically right rather than what is immediately profitable.
- *Relying on acquisitions.* Companies that build their growth plans on acquisitions rather than innovation are suspect. Half of a company's acquisitions will become tomorrow's spin-offs.
- *Middle-of-the-road strategy.* What happens to those who have a middle-of-the-road strategy? They get run over.
- *Believing if it isn't broke, don't fix it.* That is one of the worst rules of management. **"In today's economy, if it ain't broke, you might as well break it yourself, because it soon will be."** (Wayne Calloway, CEO of PepsiCo)

The sad fact is that most companies are tactics-rich and strategy-poor. Sun Tzu in the fourth century B.C. observed: **"All men can see these tactics whereby I conquer, but what none can see is the strategy out of which victory is evolved."**[58]

Success and Failure

J. Paul Getty, the fabulously wealthy founder of Getty Oil, shared his three secrets for success: **"Rise early, work late, strike oil."** Too many of us can only do the first two.

Irving Berlin, the songwriter, lamented: "The toughest thing about success is that you've got to keep on being a success." **"Success is never final,"** as Winston Churchill observed.

Success, in fact, is the major cause of failure. Five years of success will ruin any business. Lew Platt, former CEO of Hewlett-Packard, confessed: **"The single biggest problem in business is staying with your previously successful business model . . . one year too long."**

The success of a company depends ultimately on the success of its customers and partners. But a company should not try to please everyone. That would be a sure way to fail.

Failure shouldn't be viewed as always bad. Henry Ford said: **"Failure is only the opportunity to begin again more intelligently."** He added that he wouldn't hire anyone who has never failed. Thomas Huxley, the English biologist, concurred: **"There is the greatest practical benefit in making a few failures early in life."**

uppliers

The company's marketers should be interested in the company's suppliers, not just its distributors and dealers. One reason is to make sure that the company's purchasing people buy quality supplies so that the company can deliver its promised quality level to its target customers. Another reason is that undependable suppliers can lead to production delays and therefore to broken delivery promises to customers. A third reason is that good suppliers will provide value-adding ideas to the company beyond simply supplying the product.

Although the company's purchasing people should seek the best suppliers, they also are judged by their ability to keep company procurement costs down. This pressure can lead to compromises in the choice of suppliers. When Ignatio Lopez ran General Motors' procurement, he treated the suppliers harshly, always demanding a rock-bottom price even if this put some suppliers on the edge of survival. This is shortsighted. One can guess that these hard-pressed suppliers would favor the other auto companies when it came to handling shortages or unveiling innovations.

Today most companies are reducing the number of their suppliers. The thought is that one good supplier is better than three average ones. Some companies have chosen to work with a prime supplier rather than playing off suppliers against each other in the hope of gaining concessions. The auto industry has moved toward using a prime supplier for seating, another for engines, another for braking systems, and so on. These prime suppliers are treated as partners who coinvest in the success of the customer.

And if you are supplier, be thankful when you have a demanding customer. Rolls-Royce calls Boeing "the toughest customer we have" and they're grateful for it. By meeting the standards of a demanding customer, the company finds it much easier to satisfy their less demanding customers.

Target Markets

The age of companies aiming at the mass market is coming to an end. Someone said, **"Mass marketing is putting the product in the market, and going to mass on Sunday and praying someone buys it."**

Mass marketing requires developing a picture of the average customer. But averages are deceiving. If you have one foot in boiling water and another in ice water, on the average you're comfortable. If you aim for the average, you will lose.

Today many companies are trying to sell products and services to the "small business market." So they hire an ad agency to develop a mass market campaign to small businesses, with little success. It would be better to focus on a specific industry or profession and to reach the corresponding small businesses through someone who has a standing in that industry or profession. Intuit Inc. sells its small business software programs not directly but by giving a sales commission to accountants who recommend Intuit's software to small business clients.

Your company does not belong in any market where it can't be the best. John Bogle, founder of the Vanguard mutual fund company, said, **"We've never wanted to be the biggest, but the best."**

In choosing a market, remember: It is easier to sell to people with money than to people without money. And try to sell to users, not buyers.

Technology

Every new technology is a force for "creative destruction." Your company is more likely to be buried by a new technology than by its current competitors. Horse-drawn carriage makers were not defeated by a better horse-drawn carriage but by the horseless carriage. Transistors hurt the vacuum-tube industry, xerography hurt the carbon paper business, and the digital camera will hurt the film business.

New technology can also change social relations and lifestyles.

The contraceptive pill, for example, was a factor leading to smaller families, more working wives, and larger discretionary income—resulting in higher expenditures on vacation travel, durable goods, and luxury items.

New technologies will hopefully increase productivity at a greater rate than their cost. But avoid adding a new technology to an old organization. This will only result in an expensive old organization.

Telemarketing and Call Centers

Using the phone to hear from customers and to talk with customers can be a great asset if done right. Not only can you learn more about each customer but the conversation can leave the customer with a feeling of being well served. Done right, telemarketers can pick up new ideas from customers, carry out surveys to learn about the market, and even cross-sell other items.

Lands End does it right. About 85 percent of their orders come in by phone. New operators are given 75 hours of training before going on the job. Customers can phone 24 hours a day, and Lands End can answer 90 percent of the calls within 10 seconds. Overflow calls are routed to stand-by operators working at home. And customers who use Lands End's web site can also reach a live operator just by clicking an icon on their computer screens.

Unfortunately, most companies don't run their phone service in this enlightened way. Companies have rushed to automate their phone service and remove any human interface. One calls and hears a digital voice offering nine different choices, followed by another four choices, followed by three choices. And very often, the phone line is busy (because the company refuses to have enough terminals or operators), or one is put on a long waiting line before hearing a human voice. And the human voice half the time is tired, curt, or bored.

One airline goes so far as to disconnect its waiting customers after 59 minutes, all because the manager is compensated based on the average time required to handle customer calls. Can you imagine waiting 59 minutes and then being disconnected, and the impact of this experience on customer feelings toward the company?

There is a legitimate issue of how much time to spend on the phone with a customer who tends to be talkative. Most companies have trained their telemarketers how to handle a talkative person with grace. Aim essentially for customer satisfaction, not for phone speed.

Management should let telemarketers know that their conversations will be monitored. The purpose is to make sure that customers are treated respectfully and to learn best practices from the better telemarketers. Beyond this, some companies ask their executives to do some telemarketing to sense its power and problems.

Telemarketing in the future must move from one-way sales pitches to two-way conversations; from cold calls to efforts at relationship building; and from knowing nothing about the prospect to making targeted, meaningful offers.

Trends in Marketing Thinking and Practice

Here are the main marketing trends that I see:

- *From make-and-sell marketing to sense-and-respond marketing.* Your company will perform better if you view the marketing challenge as that of developing a superior understanding of your customer needs rather than as simply pushing out your products better.
- *From focusing on customer attraction to focusing on customer retention.* Companies need to pay more attention to serving and satisfying their present customers before they venture in an endless race to find new customers. Companies must move from transaction marketing to relationship marketing.
- *From pursuing market share to pursuing customer share.* The best way to grow your market share is to grow your customer share, namely to find more products and services that can be sold to the same customers.
- *From marketing monologue to customer dialogue.* You can create stronger relationships with customers by listening to and conversing with them than by only sending out one-way messages.

- *From mass marketing to customized marketing.* The mass market is splintering into mini-markets and your company now has the capability of marketing to one customer at a time.
- *From owning assets to owning brands.* Many companies are beginning to prefer owning brands to owning factories. By owning fewer physical assets and outsourcing production, these companies believe they can make a greater return.
- *From operating in the marketplace to operating in cyberspace.* Smart companies are developing a presence online as well as off-line. They are using the Internet for buying, selling, recruiting, training, exchanging, and communicating.
- *From single-channel marketing to multichannel marketing.* Companies no longer rely on one channel to reach and serve all their customers. Their customers have different preferred channels for accessing the company's products and services.
- *From product-centric marketing to customer-centric marketing.* The sign of marketing maturity is when a company stops focusing on its products and starts focusing on its customers.

These trends will affect different industries and companies at different rates and times. Your company must decide where it stands with respect to each marketing trend.

Value

The marketing job is to create, deliver, and capture customer value.

What is value? Value primarily is the putting together of the right combination of quality, service, and price (QSP) for the target market. Louis J. De Rose, head of De Rose and Associates, Inc., says: **"Value is the satisfaction of customer requirements at the lowest possible cost of acquisition, ownership, and use."**

Michael Lanning holds that winning companies are those that develop a competitively superior *value proposition* and a superior *value-delivery system.* A value proposition goes beyond the company's positioning on a single attribute. It is the sum total of the experience that the product promises to deliver backed up by the faithful delivery of this experience.

Jack Welch put this challenge to GE: **"The value decade is upon us. If you can't sell a top quality product at the world's lowest price, you're going to be out of the game."**

McDonald's used to say that it is in the *fast food business.* Later it said that it is in the *quick service business.* Today it says that it is in the *value business.*

A company's ability to deliver value to its customers is closely tied with its ability to create satisfaction for its employees and other stakeholders.

Value ultimately depends on the perceiver. A child came upon three masons and asked, "What are you doing?" "I'm mixing mortar," said the first. "I'm helping fix this wall," said the second. The third one smiled: "We're building a cathedral."

Smart companies not only offer *purchase value* but also offer *use value* as well. You invest $30,000 in an automobile and you expect the dealer to help with respect to maintenance, repair, and answering a host of questions. Ryder, the truck leasing company, not only rents a truck but provides a free book on how to pack and move. Nestlé not only sells baby food but has a 7/24 service to answer parents' questions about baby food.

Companies worry about spending more money to satisfy their customers. They need to distinguish between *value-adding costs* and *non-value-adding costs*. A hotel may consider adding afternoon bed-turning service that would raise the cost per room by $2. Before doing this, it should survey whether its customers would be willing to pay $2 for this service. If the answer is no, then bed-turning service is a non-value-adding cost. But if the hotel puts an ironing board and iron in each room at a cost of $2 and guests think it is worth $3, then this would be a value-adding cost.

Word of Mouth

No ad or salesperson can convince you about the virtues of a product as persuasively as can a friend, acquaintance, past customer, or independent expert. Suppose you are planning to buy a PDA (personal digital assistant) and you have seen all the ads for Palm, HP, and Sony. You even go to examine them at Circuit City and listen to the salesperson. You're still undecided and don't buy. Then a friend tells you how Palm has changed her life. That does it. Or you read a column by an expert who tested and describes each one and recommends Palm.

Companies would love to trigger word-of-mouth campaigns surrounding their new product launches. High-tech firms send their new products to well-respected experts and opinion leaders praying for strong editorial endorsements. Hollywood hopes for a good Roger Ebert review.

Marketers advertise their new product's benefits hoping that they would be believed and carried by word of mouth. But few know how to use experts and their customers to bring in new customers. According to word-of-mouth expert Michael Cafferky: **"Word of mouth . . . marches proudly but quietly onward as its Madison Avenue cousins try in vain to replicate its dramatic results. . . .**

Word of mouth is the brain's low-tech method of sorting through all the high-tech hype that comes to it from the market place."

Companies have been turning increasingly to word-of-mouth marketing. They seek to identify individuals who are early adopters, vocal and curious, and with a large network of acquaintances. When a company brings its new product to the attention of such influentials, the influentials carry on the rest of the work as "unpaid salespeople."

Some companies hire people to parade their new products in public areas. Someone might park a new Ferrari at a busy intersection. A stranger might ask you to take her picture; she hands you a new phone with a built-in camera, leading to an immediate conversation. Someone in a bar answers his new videophone, and everyone wants to know more about it. In March 1999, the *Blair Witch* filmmakers hired 100 college students to distribute missing person flyers in youth culture hubs to promote the film.

Today we see the rise of "aggregated buzz" in such forms as Zagat, which collects New York restaurant reviews from diners (not restaurant critics) or epinions, where people voice their opinions of products. Soon consumers will be able to tell the good guys from the bad guys and no longer have to rely on advertising.

Zest

There are two reasons to include zest in this marketing lexicon. The first, and more important, reason is that a Z word is necessary to justify the book's title.

The second is that a marketer cannot be effective without zest. Zest is defined as hearty enjoyment, gusto, enthusiasm for life. This attitude is epitomized by the way certain CEOs practiced their marketing. One is Richard Branson of Virgin, to whom marketing is the fun of creating new, better, and more satisfying solutions for people as they interact with everyday products and services. Another is Herb Kelleher, the former CEO of Southwest Airlines, who thoroughly enjoyed working at his airline and hired only people who would similarly enjoy making customers happy. Hire only marketers who have a zest for life. Otherwise send them into accounting.

Notes

1. Lester Wunderman, *Being Direct: Making Advertising Pay* (New York: Random House, 1996).
2. Peter F. Drucker, *Management: Tasks, Responsibilities, Practices* (New York: Harper & Row, 1973), pp. 64–65.
3. See Rolf Jensen, *The Dream Society: How the Coming Shift from Information to Imagination Will Transform Your Business* (New York: McGraw-Hill, 1999).
4. See David Ogilvy, *Confessions of an Advertising Man* (New York: Atheneum, 1988).
5. Ibid.
6. See Stan Rapp and Thomas L. Collins, *Beyond MaxiMarketing: The New Power of Caring and Daring* (New York: McGraw-Hill, 1994).
7. Sergio Zyman, *The End of Advertising As We Know It* (New York: John Wiley & Sons, forthcoming—2003).
8. Regis McKenna, *Total Access: Giving Customers What They Want in an Anytime, Anywhere World* (Boston: Harvard Business School Press, 2002).
9. Heidi F. Schultz and Don E. Schultz, "Why the Sock Puppet Got Sacked," *Marketing Management* (July–August 2001), pp. 35–39.

10. Richard D'Aveni with Robert Gunther, *Hypercompetitive Rivalries: Competing in Highly Dynamic Environments* (New York: Free Press, 1995).

11. Thomas H. Davenport and John C. Beck, *The Attention Economy: Understanding the New Currency of Business* (Boston: Harvard Business School Press, 2001).

12. Thomas J. Peters and Robert H. Waterman Jr., *In Search of Excellence: Lessons from America's Best-Run Companies* (New York: Harper & Row, 1982).

13. James C. Collins and Jerry I. Porras, *Built to Last: Successful Habits of Visionary Companies* (New York: HarperBusiness, 1994).

14. Michael Treacy and Fred Wiersema, *The Discipline of Market Leaders: Choose Your Customers, Narrow Your Focus, Dominate Your Market* (Reading, Mass.: Addison-Wesley, 1995).

15. Arie De Geus, *The Living Company* (Boston: Harvard Business School Press, 1997).

16. Jim Collins, *Good to Great: Why Some Companies Make the Leap . . . and Others Don't* (New York: HarperBusiness, 2001).

17. See Michael E. Porter, *Competitive Strategy: Techniques for Analyzing Industries and Competitors* (New York: Free Press, 1980); and see his *Competitive Advantage: Creating and Sustaining Superior Performance* (New York: Free Press, 1985).

18. Theodore Levitt, *The Marketing Mode: Pathways to Corporate Growth* (New York: McGraw-Hill, 1969).

19. Anita Roddick, *Body and Soul: Profits with Principles, the Amazing Success Story of Anita Roddick and the Body Shop* (New York: Crown, 1991).

20. Gregory S. Carpenter and Kent Nakamoto, "Consumer Preference Formation and Pioneering Advantage," *Journal of Marketing Research* (August 1989), pp. 285–298.

21. Jan Carlzon, *Moments of Truth* (Cambridge, Mass.: Ballinger Pub. Co., 1987).

22. Drucker, op. cit.

23. Richard Forsyth, "Six Major Impediments to Change and How to Overcome Them in CRM," *CRM-Forum* (June 11, 2001).

24. Frederick Newell, *Why CRM Doesn't Work: The Coming Empowerment Revolution in Customer Relationship Management* (New York: Bloomberg Press, forthcoming—2003).

25. See Frederick Reichheld, *The Loyalty Effect: The Hidden Force Behind Growth, Profits, and Lasting Value* (Boston: Harvard Business School Press, 1996).

26. Appeared in www.1-to-1marketing.com online. Also see Don Peppers and Martha Rogers, *The One to One Future: Building Relationships One Customer at a Time* (New York: Currency/Doubleday, 1993).

27. Seth Godin, *Permission Marketing: Turning Strangers into Friends, and Friends into Customers* (New York: Simon & Schuster, 1999).

28. Theodore Levitt, "Marketing Success through Differentiation of Anything," *Harvard Business Review* (January–February 1980), pp. 83–91.

29. Jack Trout with Steve Rivkin, *Differentiate or Die: Survival in Our Era* (New York: John Wiley & Sons, 2000).

30. Gregory S. Carpenter, Rashi Glazer, and Kent Nakamoto, "Meaningful Brands from Meaningless Differentiation: The Dependence on Irrelevant Attributes," *Journal of Marketing Research* (August 1994), pp. 339–350.

31. Hal Rosenbluth, *The Customer Comes Second: and Other Secrets of Exceptional Service* (New York: Morrow, 1992).

32. John P. Kotter and James L. Heskett, *Corporate Culture and Performance* (New York: Free Press, 1992).

33. B. Joseph Pine II and James H. Gilmore, *The Experience Economy: Work Is Theatre and Every Business a Stage* (Boston: Harvard Business School Press, 1999).

34. Hermann Simon, *Hidden Champions* (Boston: Harvard Business School Press, 1996).

35. Adrian J. Slywotzky and Richard Wise, "The Growth Crisis—and How to Escape It," *Harvard Business Review* (July 2002), pp. 73–83.

36. See Philip Kotler, *Marketing Management*, 11th edition (Upper Saddle River, N.J.: Prentice Hall, 2003), pp. 685ff.

37. See Jean-Philippe Deschamps and P. Ranganath Nayak, *Product Juggernauts: How Companies Mobilize to Generate a Stream of Market Winners* (Boston: Harvard Business School Press, 1995).

38. See Gary Hamel, *Leading the Revolution* (Boston: Harvard Business School Press, 2000).

39. See Akio Morita, *Made in Japan: Akio Morita and Sony* (New York: Dutton, 1986).

40. See James Champy, *Good to Great: Why Some Companies Make the Leap—and Others Don't* (New York: HarperBusiness, 2001).

41. Howard R. Bowen, *Social Responsibilities of the Businessman* (New York: Harper & Row, 1953), p. 215.

42. Robert Lauterborn, "New Marketing Litany: 4P's Passe; C-Words Take Over," *Advertising Age* (October 1, 1990), p. 26.

43. Paco Underhill, *Why We Buy: The Science of Shopping* (New York: Simon & Schuster, 1999).

44. Ernest Dichter, *Handbook of Consumer Motivations: The Psychology of the World of Objects* (New York: McGraw-Hill, 1964).

45. See Kevin Lane Keller, *Strategic Brand Management* (Upper Saddle River, N.J.: Prentice Hall, 1998), pp. 317–318.

46. Rosabeth Moss Kanter, *When Giants Learn to Dance* (New York: Simon & Schuster, 1989).

47. Al Ries and Jack Trout, *Positioning: The Battle for Your Mind* (New York: Warner Books, 1982).

48. Michael Treacy and Fred Wiersema, *The Discipline of Market Leaders* (Reading, Mass.: Addison-Wesley, 1994).

49. Fred Crawford and Ryan Mathews, *The Myth of Excellence: Why Great Companies Never Try to Be the Best at Everything* (New York: Crown Business, 2001).

50. Carl Sewell and Paul B. Brown, *Customers for Life: How to Turn That One-Time Buyer into a Lifetime Customer* (New York: Doubleday, 1990).
51. Ram Charan and Noel M. Tichy, *Every Business Is a Growth Business: How Your Company Can Prosper Year after Year* (New York: Times Business/Random House, 1998).
52. Al and Laura Ries, *The Fall of Advertising and the Rise of PR* (New York: HarperBusiness, 2002).
53. See the 1998 PIMS study reported in *CampaignLive*, May 3, 1999, Haymarket Publishing, U.K.).
54. Quoted in "Trade Promotion: Much Ado about Nothing," *Promo* (October 1991), p. 37.
55. See Hanish Pringle and Marjorie Thompson, *Brand Soul: How Cause-Related Marketing Builds Brands* (New York: John Wiley & Sons, 1999); Richard Earle, *The Art of Cause Marketing* (Lincolnwood, Ill.: NTC, 2000).
56. See the discussion of sponsorship in Sergio Zyman, *The End of Advertising As We Know It* (New York: John Wiley & Sons, forthcoming—2003).
57. Michael E. Porter, "What Is Strategy?" *Harvard Business Review* (November–December 1996), pp. 61–78.
58. Sun Tzu, *The Art of War* (London: Oxford University Press, 1963).

Index

A&P, 17
Accountants/accounting department, role of, 101, 104–105
Account managers, in B2B, 15
Acquisitions, 71, 174
Activities, interests, and opinions (AIOs), 43
Actors, in marketing plan, 112
Advertising:
  aim of, 2, 18–19
  brand development and, 9, 161
  budget, 3, 6–7, 145
  competition and, 23
  creativity in, 2–3
  customer satisfaction in, 42
  defined, 2
  development process, 2, 4
  development software, 82
  effectiveness of, 6–7
  five Ms of, 4–5
  limitations of, 7–8
  measurement, 6–7
  media selection, 4–5
  message text, 5
  product life cycle and, 110
  sales promotion, 160–162
  successful campaigns, examples of, 3–4
  wear-out, 1–2
Advertising agency:
  budget, 7
  functions of, 2, 4–5
  pay-for-performance basis, 63
Alberto Culver, 51
Allied Van Lines, 75
Amazon.com, 12, 84, 146, 155
American Airlines, 33

American Express, 14, 71
America Online (AOL), 86
Analytics, 80–82
Anchoring, 29
Annual-plan control, 78
Apple Computer, 9, 12, 47–48, 93, 97, 127, 142
Armstrong, J. S., 121
Armstrong World Industries, Inc., 72
Asea Brown Boveri (ABB), 88
Asset turnover, 62, 69
AT&T, 72
A. T. Cross, 74
Atimex, 170
Attention Economy, The (Davenport/Beck), 19
Attribute listing, 28
Audits, 79, 115
Avis, 137

Balance sheets, 62
Bang & Olufsen, 47–48
Barnes & Noble, 84, 93, 154, 156
Bass Pro, 62
Battle plan, *see* Marketing plans
Baum, Herbert, 118
Bayer, 12
BBBK Pest Control, 75
Beanie Babies, 146
Becher, 66
Beck, John, 19
Behavior groups, 163
Being alive, 29
Benefit marketing, 76
Bernbach, William, 1
Berra, Yogi, 67, 70

Best Buy, 155
Best practices, 155
Beyond MaxiMarketing (Rapp/Collins), 7
Bezos, Jeff, 14, 59, 109, 139
Big Five accounting firms, 137
Big Three auto firms, 137
Black & Decker, 12
Blackberry, 146
BMW, 97, 135
Body Shop, The, 31, 146
Boeing, 20, 177
Bogle, John, 178
Borders, 55–56, 154
Bossidy, Larry, 59, 71
Brainstorming, 29–30, 84
Branch offices, global expansion, 88
Brand(s):
    advertising and, 9–10
    attributes of, 10–11
    benefits of, 10
    building models, 13-14
    development process, 9–12, 146
    differentiation, 49
    extension, defined, 11–13
    importance of, 8
    line extension and, 11–13
    loyalty and, 8–9, 97
    management of, 13
    name selection, 10, 12
    personality, 11, 27
    preference for, 8–9
    pricing strategies, 13
    stretch, 11
    successful, 11
    value, 86
Brand-customer relationship, 10
Branding, 7
Brand management myopia, 13
Brand manager, role of, 82, 161
Branson, Richard, 10, 12, 187
Braun, 83
Brighthouse, 28
British Airways, 57
Britt, Dr. Steuart Henderson, 3
Budget:
    advertising, 3, 6–7, 145
    financial marketing, 62
    marketing plan, 113, 149
Built to Last (Collins/Porras), 21
Burger King, 10
Burnett, Leo, 2, 28
Business cards, 125
Business-to-business (B2B) marketing,
    15–16, 65
Business-to-consumer (B2C) marketing, 15
Butler, Nicholas Murray, 168

Cadillac, 10
Cafferky, Michael, 185

Call centers, 179–180
Campbell Soup, 11
Capital market, 84
Carlzon, Jan, 32
Carpenter, Greg, 31, 50
Cash flow statements, 62
Cashing out, 29, 128
Casio, 83
Catalogs, 52
Category killers, 154
Caterpillar, 20, 26–27
Cathay Pacific, 23
Celebrity spokespeople, 7, 169–170
CEO, *see* Chief executive officer (CEO)
Chambers, John, 92
Champion, 87
Change, importance of, 16–18, 122. *See also*
    Innovation; New product development
Channel conflict, 54–55
Channel relationships, 87
Chapman, Harry, 100
Charan, Ram, 143
Charles Schwab, 56
Chief executive officer (CEO):
    brand development, 14
    customer orientation, 32
    financial marketing, 63
    marketing role, 119
    success factors, 94–96
Chief financial officer (CFO), 95–96
Chief operating officer (COO), functions of,
    94
Churchill, Winston, 95, 175
Circuit City, 155
Cisco Systems, 14, 59
Citicorp, 72
Clanning, 29
Club Med, 84
Club membership, benefits of, 9, 40
CNN, 84
Coach, 87
Coca-Cola, 1, 6, 8, 12–13, 23, 47, 72, 86,
    107, 140, 169
Cocooning, 29, 128
Cold calls, 180
Collins, Jim, 21
Collins, Thomas, 7
Command-and-control economies,
    122
Communication(s):
    defined, 18
    in 4Cs, 109
    integrated marketing communications
        (IMC), 18
    Internet and, 91–92
    promotion, 18–19
    relationship marketing, 153
    sales force, 159
    team guidelines, 105–106

Companies, generally:
  size of, 20–21, 111
  success factors, 21
  types of, 20
Competitive advantage, 22–23, 56, 59,
  76
Competitors:
  awareness of, 24
  customer needs and, 31
  customer service and, 24
  effective, 24
  positioning and, 136
  sales promotions, 111
  shift to, 150
  successful companies and, 23
  types of, 23
Complaint handling strategies, 40
Computer software programs:
  CRM-Forum, 35
  database marketing, generally, 104
  development of, 82
  marketing automation software, 81
  marketing process automation, 82
  marketing strategy simulators, 114
  partner relationship management (PRM),
    55
  real-time inventory management, 81
  real-time selling, 81–82
  sales automation software, 80–81
  supply chain software, 104
  types of, generally, 82
Concept test, 82
Consultants, 25–26
Consumer marketers, 111
Consumer packaged goods (CPG):
  brand building process, 13–14
  customer service, 42
Consumer panels, 115
Continuous improvement, 84, 144
Contract management, 82
Controls:
  distribution/channels, 54–55
  efficiency, 79
  financial marketing, 63
  in marketing plan, 113
  profitability, 79
  strategic, 79
Convenience, importance of, 109
Copyrights, 86
Core competencies, 101, 132
Core processes, 101
Corporate branding, 26–27. *See also* Brands
Corporate Culture and Performance
  (Kotter/Heskett), 59
Corporate growth:
  examples of, 72
  goal-setting, 69
  opportunities for, 73
  strategies for, 70–72

Corporate image, 27. *See also* Image;
  Reputation
Costco, 154
Cost-cutting strategies:
  overview, 63–64, 71, 143
  recession marketing, 150
Cost of capital, 63
Countertrading, 90
Crawford, Fred, 137
Creativity:
  development strategies, 27–28
  idea markets, 29–30
  importance of, 27
  techniques, 28–29
  trend spotters, 29
  uniqueness, 27–28
Credit department, 104
CRM-Forum, 35
Cross-selling, 34–35
Customer(s), generally:
  acquisition of, 37–38, 41
  advocacy, 14
  attraction, 181
  awareness of, 37, 39
  base, value of, 86
  classification system, 40
  compensation systems, 38–39
  complaints from, 40
  corporate growth, role in, 73
  costs, 109
  defection rate, 41
  defined, 37
  dialogue, 181
  experience, 137
  intimacy, 137
  life cycle, 37
  lifetime value, 37
  loyalty, 3, 8–9, 13, 42, 98, 161,
    170
  loyalty award program, 98
  needs, 30–31, 39, 73
  new product development process,
    127
  orientation, 32–34
  perceptions of, 36–38
  power of, 59
  privacy issues, 45–46
  relationships, 39, 87
  retention, *see* Customer retention
  satisfaction, 3, 14, 21, 38–39, 41–42
Customer-centered companies, 33–34
Customer-centric marketing,
  182
Customer-driven companies, 21
Customer management of relationships
  (CMR), 36
Customer managers, 33
Customer-oriented companies, 33, 131
Customer-owning focus, 36

Customer relationship management (CRM),
   see Database marketing
   benefits of, generally, 36
   components of, 35–36
   defined, 13, 34
   effectiveness of, 35
Customer retention:
   focus on, 181
   implications of, 14, 42
   strategies for, 38, 41
Customer service:
   complaint handling strategies,
      40
   functions of, 105
   importance of, 7, 23
   quality of, 168
Customers for Life (Sewell), 141
Customer share:
   implications of, 37, 109, 181
   value proposition, 150
Customized marketing, 182

Dana Corporation, 85
Database marketing:
   benefits of, 44–45
   customer privacy and, 45–46
   data collection strategies, 43–44
   defined, 39
   effectiveness factors, 45
   updating information, 44
Data collection strategies, 43–44
Data mining, 44, 118
D'Aveni, Richard, 17
Davenport, Thomas, 19
Dealers, creativity and, 29
Decapitalization, 87
Decision trees, 29
De Geus, Arie, 21, 82
Delivery, competition and, 23. *See also*
   Distribution/channels
Dell Computer, 42, 56, 84, 93, 107, 124,
   144
Delta Air Lines, 32–33
Demand flow, 81
Deming, W. Edwards, 147
Demographics/demographic groups, 35, 43,
   163
De Rose, Louis J., 183
Design:
   criteria for, 47
   service businesses and, 48
   style distinguished from, 46–47
   target customer, identification of,
      48
   types of, 46
   value-added products, 48
Developing countries, 88–89
Dichter, Ernest, 117
Differentiate or Die (Trout), 50

Differentiation:
   commodities and, 49–50
   development strategies, 50–51
   importance of, 50
   types of, 49–50
Direct mail, 52
Discipline of Market Leaders, The
   (Treacy/Wiersema), 21
Discontinuous innovation, 84
Disney, 33, 59, 84, 107
Disney, Walt, 57, 61
Distribution/channels:
   channel conflict, 54–55
   channel partners, 55–56
   customer reward programs, 56
   global expansion, 88
   go-to-market, 53–54
   implications of, 56
   integrated channels, 56
   market control, 54–55
   market coverage, 54
   multiple channels, 55–56
   partner relationship management (PRM),
      55
   relationship marketing, 153
Distributors, creativity and, 29
Dollar General, 129
Domino's Pizza, 84
Dot.coms, 93
Down-aging, 29, 31, 128
Drucker, Peter, 26, 37, 54, 70, 77, 100,
   139, 144, 148, 157, 174

Earnings per share (EPS), 69
Ease of access, 137
Eastern Airlines, 33
Eastman Kodak, 20, 77–78
eBay, 9, 146
E-commerce, 93–94
Economic value added (EVA), 62–63,
   68
Efficiency control, 79
Emmperative, 82
Emotional marketing, 76–77
Employee(s):
   brand values and, 59
   compensation, 58
   creativity and, 29
   as customer, 57
   customer satisfaction and, 59–60
   growth mentality, 73
   hiring practices, 32–33, 57–58,
      187
   importance of, 57, 59
   internal marketing, 58–59
   recognition of, 59
   recruitment, 91
   relationships, 87
   service quality, 168

smile index, 168
training, 33, 179–180
value, 86
value proposition, 58
Empowerment, customer, 35–36
Engineering department, 103, 127
Entrepreneurship, 60–61
Environmental design, 46
Environsell, 115
E.piphany, 82
Estée Lauder, 162
Events, brand development and, 9
Every Business Is a Growth Business: How Your Company Can Prosper Year after Year (Charan/Tichy), 143
Experiential marketing, 61–62
Exporting, 88–89

Failure, influential factors, 175
Fall of Advertising and the Rise of PR, The (Ries/Ries), 146
Fans, customers as, 38
Fantasy adventure, 29
Fay, Christopher, 139
Federal Express, 2, 84, 107
Feed forward/feed back system, 79
Ferragamo, 2
Ferrari, 2
Ferris, Dick, 96
Finance department, 103
Financial marketing:
    CEO role in, 63
    components of, generally, 62–63
    marketing controllers, 63
    marketing effectiveness, 64
    marketing efficiency, 63
Financing, competition and, 23
FitzGerald, Niall, 9
Focus groups, 115–116
Focusing, 64–66
Forbes 100, 20
Forced relationships, 28
Ford, 20, 37, 106
Ford, Henry, 175
Forecasting, 66–68
4Cs, 109
4Ps, 108–109
Free cash flow, 62
Frequency, in advertising campaign, 5
Frequent-flier programs, 98
Fujitsu, 23

Gabor, Dennis, 68
Gardner, John, 128
Gates, Bill, 24, 92
General Electric, 14, 20, 59, 93, 104, 107, 133

General Motors, 20, 136, 147, 173
Gerstner, Lou, 96
Getty, J. Paul, 175
Giant retailers, 154–155
Gillette, 48, 50
Gilmore, James, 61
Glazer, Rashi, 50
Globalization, impact of, 139
Goals:
    importance of, 68
    incentive programs and, 135
    types of, 69–70
Godin, Seth, 46
Goizueta, Roberto, 8, 23, 72
Golden Rule of Marketing, 38
Good to Great: Why Some Companies Make the Leap . . . and Others Don't (Collins), 21
Gorillas, in niching, 64–65
Go-to-market strategy:
    alternatives to, 53–54
    defined, 53
Graham, Katherine, 95
Graphics/graphic design, 27, 46
Grove, Andrew, 16, 100
Growth strategies, 70–73
Guarantees, 74–75
Gucci, 2
Guerrilla marketing, 64–65
Guido, Pietro, 30

Hamel, Gary, 58, 83–84, 143
Hampton Inn, 74
Hanes, 87
Hanlin, Russell, 8
Hard Rock Café, 61
Harkness, Richard, 100
Harley Davidson, 9, 27, 38, 97, 137, 141, 172
Heinz, 12
Henderson, Bruce, 141, 171
Hertz, 170
Heskett, Jim, 59
Hewlett-Packard (HP), 14, 16, 56, 107, 127, 185
Hewlett-Packard/Compaq iPAQ Pocket PC, 12, 47
Hidden assets, 73
Hidden Champions (Simon), 65
Hillshire Farms, 87
Hock, Dee, 173
Holiday Inn, 42
Holistic marketing, 119–120
Home Depot, 71, 155
Honda, 42, 83
HP/Compaq, 93
Hudson River Group, 114
Human resources, *see* Employee(s); Recruitment; Training programs

Huxley, Thomas, 175
Hypercompetition, 139
Hypercompetitive Rivalries (D'Aveni), 17
Hypermarkets, 154
Hyundai, 136

Iacocca, Lee, 139
IBM, 23, 40, 49, 93, 107, 122, 158,
  165
Idea manager, role of, 85
Idea markets, 29–30, 84
IKEA, 22, 27, 84, 129, 132, 137,
  172
Image:
  brand, 156, 162
  differentiation strategies, 51
  importance of, 76–77
Impact, in advertising campaign, 5
Implementation:
  buy-in, 78
  problems with, 77–78
Incentive programs, 59, 135
Income statements, 62
Industry-oriented companies, 131
Industry par, 137
Information exchange systems, global
  expansion, 89
Information gathering, *see* Data collection
  strategies
Information management, 80–82
Information technology (IT) department,
  104
Innovation:
  importance of, 31, 83–85
  index, 85
In Search of Excellence (Peters/Waterman),
  21
Inside-out thinking, 73
Intangible assets, 86–87
Integrated channels, 56
Integrated marketing communications
  (IMC), 18
Intel, 16, 59, 107
Intellectual capital value, 86–87
Internal marketing, 17, 58–59
International expansion, 71
International marketing:
  benefits of, 87
  brand name, 87–88
  developing countries, 89
  development stages, 88
  failure factors, 90
  management, 89
  market share, 89
  troubled countries, 89–90
Internet:
  benefits of, 91–93, 182
  corporate web site, 94
  e-commerce, 93–94

pricing strategy, impact on, 139
  retail industry, impact on, 155
Interviews, market research, 117–118
Intranet, 92
Inventory management, 81

Jaguar, 46–47
Japanese strategies:
  customer needs, 30
  innovation, 83–84
  inventory management, 81
  marketing departments, 130
  market research, 116
  performance measurement, 133
  profit/profitability objectives, 144–145
  quality management, 147–148
J. D. Powers, 42
Johnson & Johnson, 8, 65, 107,
  125
J. P. Morgan, 20
Junk mail, 46, 52

Kaizen, 100
Kamprad, Ingvard, 127
Kanter, Rosabeth Moss, 99, 129
Kelleher, Herb, 59, 187
Kellogg, 20
Kmart, 17, 149
Knowledge:
  management, 80
  value of, 86
Kotter, John, 59
Kraft, 141
Kumar, Nirmalya, 164, 172

Lands End, 60, 179
Lanning, Michael, 183
Lao-tzu, 95
Lauterborn, Robert, 109
Layoffs, 150
Leacock, Stephen, 2
Leadership:
  chief executive officer (CEO), 94–96
  chief financial officer (CFO), 95–96
  chief operating officer (COO), 94
  circle, 137
  effective, 95–96
  egotism and, 96
  functions of, 95
  respect for, 95
  success factors, 95–96
  vision, 95–96
Lean businesses, 87, 151
Le Carré, John, 100
Levi's, 12, 94
Levitt, Theodore, 23, 50, 140, 142,
  167
Lexus, 12–13, 83
Licenses, 86

Light, Larry, 13
Line extension, 11–13
Line management, functions of, 78, 89
List brokers, 124
Living Company, The (De Geus), 21
L. L. Bean, 33, 37, 75
Loblaws, 74, 156
Logos, 27
Lopez, Ignatio, 176
Lowe's, 155
Low-price firms, 144
Loyalty:
  brand, 97
  customer, 98
  defined, 97
Loyalty award program, 98

McDonald's, 84, 116, 124–125, 183
McKenna, Regis, 7
Macro forces, in marketing plan, 112
Make-and-sell marketing, 181
Management:
  committees, 100–101
  core processes, 99
  functions of, generally, 99–100
  success factors, 100
Management by objectives, 70
Manufacturing department, 104, 127
Margins, 133
Market capitalization, 63
Market control, 54–55
Market coverage, 54
Market-driven companies, 21, 31
Market-driving companies, 31
Marketers, roles of, 119–121
Marketing, generally:
  ability, 121
  assets and resources, 101–102
  budget, 149
  department interfaces, 102–106
  effectiveness, 64
  efficiency, 63
  ethics, 106–107
  monologue, 181
  myopia, 140
  plans, *see* Marketing plans
  research, *see* Market research
  roles and skills, 119–121
  shootouts, 174
  strategy simulators, 114
Marketing auditor, marketing control role, 79
Marketing automation software, 81
Marketing control, types of, 78–79
Marketing controller, role of, 63, 79
Marketing department:
  interfaces, 102–106
  roles of, 127

Marketing mix:
  company size and, 11
  4Cs of, 109
  4Ps of, 108–109
  product life cycle and, 110–112
  push strategies, 111
Marketing plans:
  applications, generally, 113
  benefits of, 114
  budget, 113
  controls, 113
  deficient, 114
  implementation of, 114
  objectives, 112–113
  situational analysis, 112–113
  strategy, 113
  success factors, 114
  tactics, 113–114
Marketing process automation, 82
Market leadership, components of, 21, 31
Market life cycle, 37
Market of one, defined, 122
Market research:
  data mining, 118
  focus groups, 115–116
  importance of, 115, 118
  in-depth interviews, 117–118
  in-home observations, 116
  in-store observations, 115–116
  marketing experiments, 118
  motivational, 117
  mystery shoppers, 118
  observations, generally, 116
  questionnaires, 115, 117
  surveys, 115, 117
Markets, types of, 121–122
Market segments, defined, 162. *See also* Segmentation
Market share:
  global expansion and, 89
  importance of, 39, 41, 69
  performance measurement and, 133
  pursuit of, 181
Markups, 139
Marriott, 14, 57, 141
Mars Company, 124
Marsteller, William, 26
Mass market/marketing, 46, 121, 177–178
Mathews, Ryan, 137
Matsushita, 142
Mature markets, 71, 158
Maytag, 107
Measurement, in advertising, 4. *See also* Performance measurement
Media:
  in advertising, 4
  new product development and, 126
  types of, 122–123

Mercedes, 13, 97
Message, in advertising, 4–5
Microsoft Corporation, 9, 21, 97, 107, 142
Middle management, marketing control role, 78
Mission:
  in advertising, 4
  importance of, 124–125
Modification analysis, 28
Moments of truth, defined, 32
Moments of Truth (Carlzon), 32
Monaghan, Tom, 38
Money, in advertising, 4, 6
Montblanc, 47
Morita, Akio, 30, 84–85
Morphological analysis, 28
Most Growable Customers (MGCs), 40
Most Profitable Customers (MPCs), 40
Most Troubling Customers (MTCs), 40
Most Vulnerable Customers (MVCs), 40
Multichannel marketing, 182
Multidivisional companies, 130–131
Multinational corporations, 89–90
Mystery shopper research, 118

Naisbet, John, 29
Nakamato, Kent, 31, 50
Name selection, in brand development, 10
Narrower niches, 162
National brands, 156
Need groups, 163
Nestlé, 84, 170, 184
Netscape, 127
Neutragena, 137
New Economy, 14
Newell, Frederick, 35–36
New product development:
  importance of, 71, 82, 84, 126
  outsourcing, 131–132
  success factors, 126–127
Niching, 64–66
Niebuhr, Reinhold, 18
Nike, 71–72, 76, 131, 170
Niketown, 62
99 lives, 29
No-need society, 30
No-Need Society, The (Guido), 30
Nokia, 16, 146
Non-value-adding costs, 184
Nucor, 71

Objectives:
  importance of, 68–70
  in marketing plan, 112–113
  prioritizing, 174

Observations:
  in-home, 116
  in-store, 115–116
  types of, generally, 116
Obsolete products, 23, 127
Office Depot, 155
Office Max, 155
Ogilvy, David, 3, 8
Ogilvy & Mather, 116
Olson, Ken, 67
One-to-one marketing, 44
Operational excellence, 137, 171
Opportunity, recognition of, 128–129, 150–151
Oracle, 94
O'Reilly, Tony, 98
Organization, implications of, 130–131. *See also* Companies
Organizational culture:
  employee incentives/recognition, 59, 135
  global expansion and, 88
  intrapreneurial spirit, 61
  recession marketing, 151
Organizational fat, 150
Osborn, Alex, 30
Outside-in thinking, 73
Outsourcing, 102, 131–132, 157, 182
Overfocusing, 174

Packaging, 7
Palm, 9, 12, 31, 47, 146, 185
Partner relationship management (PRM), 55
Partner value:
  defined, 86
  proposition, 150
Patents, 86
Pay-for-performance, 6, 63
PENCILS, 146
PepsiCo, 6, 90, 170
Perdue, Frank, 50
Performance measurement:
  importance of, 133–134
  sales force, 158–159
  types of, 134–135
Permission marketing, 46, 52
Personalization, 109
Personal selling, 110. *See also* Sales force
Personnel, *see* Employee(s)
Peters, Tom, 17, 21, 37, 50
Philanthropy, 170. *See also* Social causes
Physical assets, 87, 101, 182
Physical differentiation, 49
Physical evidence, marketing mix and, 108
Pierce, John R., 67
Pine, Joe, 61
Place, in 4Ps, 108–109
Planet Hollywood, 61
Platt, Lew, 175

Playtex, 87
Pleasure revenge, 29
Politics, 108
Pollard, Bill, 58
Popcorn, Faith, 28–29
Porras, Jerry, 21
Porsche, 135
Porter, Michael, 22, 171
Positioning, 135–138
Positioning: The Battle for Your Mind
  (Ries/Trout), 135
Positive-sum theory of marketing,
  142
Postmeasurements, in advertising, 6
Potter, Robert, 130
Power, Brendan, 148
Power brands, 141
Premeasurement, in advertising, 6
President's Choice, 156
Price:
  in 4Ps, characteristics of, 108–109,
    153
  in positioning strategy, 137
  relationship marketing, 153
  setting, *see* Pricing strategies
  significance of, 138–139
  value and, 138
  wars, 174
Price, Kevin, 154
Pricing strategies:
  brand development and, 13
  corporate growth and, 71
  in global expansion, 88–89
  influential factors, 139
  markup and, 139
  recession marketing, 150
Private brands, 156
Procedures, 108
Procter & Gamble, 107, 162
Product:
  awareness, 2
  design, 46
  differentiation strategies, 51
  in 4Ps, characteristics of, 108–109, 153
  leadership, 136–137
  life cycle, 110–111
  in positioning strategy,
    137
  problem analysis, 28–29
  relationship marketing, 153
  selection factors, 140
Product-centric marketing, 182
Product development, innovation process,
  83–85. *See also* New product
  development
Product directors, role of, 89
Product-driven companies, 33–34
Productivity, innovation strategies, 85
Product juggernauts, 83

Product-making focus, 36
Product-oriented companies, 130–131
Profits/profitability:
  control, 79
  cost-cutting strategies and, 143
  Japanese-formulated objectives, 144–145
  low-price firms, 144
  positive-sum theory of marketing, 142
  pricing strategies and, 144
  zero-sum thinking, 142
Promotion, *see* Advertising; Sales promotion
  defined, 18
  effectiveness of, 19
  in 4Ps, 108–111
  strategies for, 19
Protectionism, 173
Prudential, 76
Psychographics, 35, 43
Publicity, 7
Public relations (PR):
  advertising *vs.*, 145–146
  functions of, generally, 9, 12, 19, 27, 108,
    126, 146–147
  new product development, 146
  PENCILS of, 146
Pull strategies, 111
Purchasing department, 103–104, 176
Push strategies, 111

Quality:
  importance of, 127, 147–148
  Japanese perspective, 147–148
  managerial responsibility, 147
  in performance measurement,
    134
  pricing strategies and, 141–142
Quality, service, and price (QSP),
  183
Questionnaires, 115, 117
Quinn, James Brian, 114

Rapp, Stan, 7
Rawlins, Gregory, 23
Reach, in advertising campaign, 5
Real-time inventory management,
  81
Real-time selling, 81–82
Recession marketing, 149–151
Recruitment, 91, 187
Reebok, 72, 170
Reengineering, 99, 130
Reeves, Rosser, 1
Referrals, 98
Regional headquarters, global expansion,
  88–89
Regional management, functions of,
  89
REI (outdoor equipment store), 62
Relationship capital, 151

Relationship differentiation, 50
Relationship marketing (RM):
  characteristics of, 151–152
  defined, 152
  4Ps and, 153
  sales promotion and, 160
  shift to, 152–153, 154
Relationship scorecard, 151
Reputation, importance of, 69, 113
Research and development (R&D), 89, 119,
  127
Resegmentation, 72
Retail anthropologists, 115–116
Retailers, 154–156
Retailing, success factors, 155–156
Return on assets (ROA), 62
Return on investment (ROI), 62–63
Return on sales, 69
Ries, Al, 12, 135–136, 146,
  173
Ries, Laura, 146
Ritz-Carlton, 48
Roddick, Anita, 31, 57
Rogers, Martha, 44
Rolex Watch Company, 55
Rolls-Royce, 177
Roosevelt, Franklin, 95
Rosenbluth Travel, 57
Royal Ahold, 88
Ryder, 184

Sales automation software, 80–81
Sales department, functions of, 130
Sales force:
  compensation, 157–158
  functions of, generally, 105
  marketing role, 158–159
  motivation for, 158
  need for, 157
  outsourcing, 132
  performance measurement, 158–159
  sales automation equipment, 159
  strategies, *see* Sales strategies
Sales promotion, 19, 160–162
Sales strategies:
  business-to-business (B2B) marketing,
    15–16
  personal selling, 110–111
  pull strategies, 111
  push strategies, 111
  videoconferencing, 16
Sam's, 155
Sara Lee Corporation, 87
Saturn (carmaker), 75
Scandinavian Airlines System (SAS), 32
Schultz, Heidi and Don, 13
Schwab, Charles, 14
Sears, 20, 173
Sectors, segments *vs.*, 163

Segmentation:
  in corporate growth, 71–72
  types of, 162–164
Segments of one, 163
Selling:
  effective salespeople, 165–166
  images of, 164–165
  personal, 110–111
  rejection, dealing with, 165
  success factors, 165–167
  telemarketing, 179–180
  value creation, 167
Sense-and-respond marketing, 34, 181
Service, *see* Customer service
  design, 46
  differentiation strategies, 51
  importance of, 167–168
Service businesses, design considerations,
  48
7-Eleven, 81
7-Up, 137
Sewell, Carl, 141
Shareholder value, 63
Siebel, Tom, 21, 95
Siemens, 131, 148
Simon, Hermann, 65
Singapore Airlines, 23
Single-channel marketing, 182
Situational analysis, in marketing plan,
  112–113
Slywotzky, Adrian, 73
Small indulgences, 29
Smile index, 168
Social causes, participation in, 9, 169
Sony, 10, 12, 14, 26, 48, 83, 107, 142, 185
Southwest Airlines, 22, 27, 129, 132, 137,
  144, 172
Spin-offs, 174
Spokespersons, 7, 9, 169–170
Sponsorship, 7, 9, 169–170
Staff management, marketing control role,
  78
Stakeholders, 113
Stanley Works, 164–165
Staples, 155
Starbucks Coffee Company, 9, 14, 48,
  54–55, 61, 84
State Farm Mutual Automobile Insurance,
  98
Statler, Ellsworth, 168
Stead, Jerre L., 144
Steiner Optical, 65–66
Stew Leonard's, 156
Strategic control, 79
Strategic positioning, 171, 173
Strategic segment, 164
Strategy:
  bad, examples of, 173–174
  components of, 172

examples of, 172
  importance of, 171–172
  middle-of-the-road, 174
  strategic positioning, 171, 173
  value proposition, 171–172
Style, in design, 46–47
Success factors, generally, 175
Sunkist, 8
Sun Tzu, 23, 174
Superstores, 154
Suppliers:
  creativity and, 29
  importance of, 176–177
  relationships, 87
Supply chain software, 104
Surveys, in market research, 115, 117
Swatch (watchmaker), 84
SWOT (strengths, weaknesses, opportunities, threats) analysis, 112–113, 152
Synectics, 29

Taco Bell, 72
Tactical marketing, 119
Tag line, 27
Takeuchi, Hiroyuki, 130
Talent market, 84
Tamcsin, Dennis, 165
Target (stores), 149
Target customer, identification of, 48. See also Target market
Target market:
  customer research, 35–36
  defined, 122
  in global expansion, 88
  identification of, 19
  importance of, 177–178
  segmentation of, 162–163
  value proposition, 171–172
Technological advances, 178–179
Telemarketers/telemarketing, 44, 135, 159, 179–180
Television advertising, 123, 145
Tetra Food, 66
Thompson, John, 59
3M, 59, 83, 102, 107
3Vs, in strategy development, 172
Tichy, Noel M., 143
Tiffany, 2
Toffler, Alvin, 29
Top management, marketing control role, 78–79
Total product, 141
Townsend, Robert, 26, 95
Toyota, 12, 48
Toys 'R' Us, 154
Trademarks, 86
Training programs, 33, 180
Transaction history, 43
Transaction marketing (TM), 152, 154, 160

Transaction-oriented marketing, 46
Treacy, Michael, 21, 136
Trends:
  customer-centric marketing, 182
  customer dialogue, 181
  customer needs and, 31
  customer retention, focus on, 181
  customer share, pursuit of, 181
  customized marketing, 182
  cyberspace, operating in, 182
  detection strategies, 44, 122
  multichannel marketing, 182
  owning brands, 182
  sense-and-respond marketing, 181
Trend spotters, 29
Trout, Jack, 12, 50, 135–136, 173
Truman, Harry, 68, 95
Tylenol, 12

Underhill, Paco, 115–116
Unica, 82
Unilever, 80, 141
Uniqueness, 27
United Parcel Service, 107
Up-selling, 34–35
USAA, 65

Value, generally:
  creation, 167
  defined, 183
  disciplines, 136
  network, 172
  perception of, 184
  proposition, see Value proposition
  purchase, 184
  target, 172
  use, 184
Value-added, generally:
  products, 48
  service, 137
Value-adding costs, 184
Value-delivery system, 183–184
Value proposition:
  customer, 150
  defined, 183
  importance of, 58, 98, 172
  partner, 150
Vendors, 154–156
Venture capital, 94
Vertical organizations, 130
Viagra, 9, 126, 146
Videoconferencing, 16
Vigilant consumers, 29
Virgin Atlantic Airways, 125
Virgin brand, 10, 12, 26
Virtual organizations, 132
Vision, importance of, 95, 112
Volvo, 135, 138

Walgreen, Charles R., III, 95
Walgreen Co., 95
Wal-Mart, 22, 71, 81, 84, 93, 129, 132,
     137, 144, 149
Walton, Sam, 59–60, 168
Wanamaker, John, 4
Warehouse withdrawals, 115
Warehousing, competition and, 23
Waterman, Bob, 21
Watson, Thomas J., 67
Wealth creation, 147
Web sites, benefits of, 94, 156
Welch, Jack, 16–17, 38, 59, 67, 72, 92, 96,
     133, 148, 183
Western Union, 17
When Giants Learn to Dance (Kanter), 129
Whirlpool, 116
Why We Buy (Underhill), 115
Wiersema, Fred, 21, 136
Wilson, Earl, 127

Winnebago Industries, 151
Wise, Richard, 73
Word-of-mouth campaigns, 185–186
Working capital, 81, 101
Wrigley, 44

Xerox, 12, 31, 74, 127

Zagat, 186
Zaltman, Gerald, 117
Zaltman Metaphor Elicitation Technique
     (ZMET), 117–118
Zero customer feedback time, 144
Zero defects, 145
Zero inventory, 145
Zero product improvement time,
     144
Zero-sum thinking, 142
Zest, 187
Zyman, Sergio, 7